AF428215

Strategic Negotiation in Organizational Transformation

A Practitioner's Guide to the Conversations That Determine Whether Change Succeeds

Adolfo M. Carreno

Strategic Negotiation in Organizational Transformation

A Practitioner's Guide to the Conversations That Determine Whether Change Succeeds

Adolfo M. Carreno

Published by Omou Press under license

Houston, Texas, United States of America

First edition, 2026

The scenarios, organizations, and individuals described in this book are composites or fictional constructions used for illustrative purposes. Any resemblance to actual persons, organizations, or events is coincidental.

ISBN 979-8-9955272-0-6 (paperback)

ISBN 979-8-9955272-1-3 (ebook)

10 9 8 7 6 5 4 3 2 1

Strategic Negotiation in Organizational Transformation

A Practitioner's Guide to the Conversations That Determine Whether Change Succeeds

Adolfo M. Carreno

CONTENTS

PREFACE

There is a difference between the formal description of transformation and the experience of carrying one forward. In presentations and documents, change appears orderly and structured. In practice, it settles into conversations that are far more delicate. I have spent many years working inside organizations of different sizes, in environments where expectations shift quickly and where people protect what they value with more care than any chart can capture. Over time, I learned that the success of a transformation rarely depends on the design of the plan. It depends on how well the conversations beneath the plan are handled.

This book exists because those conversations are often neglected. Many transformation efforts stall not for lack of strategy, resources, or leadership attention. They stall because interests remain unspoken, because resistance appears in subtle forms, or because groups with legitimate concerns feel unseen. The work that determines whether a program moves forward or loses momentum happens in these moments, yet many professionals enter them without the structure or language needed to navigate them well.

What this book offers is a way to understand and engage with those moments. It grew out of repeated experiences where a difficult conversation held at the right time changed the trajectory of a major program. I have seen teams unlock cooperation once their real motivations were acknowledged. I have also seen costly delays arise simply because a decision was framed in a way that caused unnecessary fear. These observations shaped my conviction that negotiation is not an external-facing skill reserved for contracts and counterparties. It is an internal leadership discipline that helps organizations move through uncertainty with steadiness.

The problem addressed here is not limited to any single industry. Transformation creates discomfort because it alters routines, identities, and balances of influence. People rarely resist the stated goal. They resist what they believe they might lose along the way. When their concerns remain unclear, alignment becomes fragile. When their interests are understood and treated seriously, cooperation becomes far more stable. This book provides a structure for identifying those interests and for using them to shape agreements that stand up to real pressures.

The intended readers are those who guide transformation from the inside. Program managers, change leaders, functional heads, senior sponsors, and anyone who carries responsibility for aligning groups that approach the same initiative from different perspectives. These readers know that resistance often appears in forms that are difficult to name. They know that formal authority reaches only so far. They have seen how much depends on conversations that unfold without public attention, guided only by the skill and judgment of the person in the room.

My aim is to offer support for that work: tools that are practical, language that is usable in real discussions, and reflections that come from lived experience rather than abstract theory. If the ideas in these pages help you approach a difficult situation with more confidence, or help you see the landscape of a transformation more clearly, then this book will have found its purpose in the place where it matters most, the quieter work of negotiation.

Adolfo M. Carreno

HOW TO USE THIS BOOK

This book has been arranged to serve readers who are already in the middle of something. Transformation work does not pause while its practitioners read about it, and the questions that matter most tend to arrive without much warning. A chapter on stakeholder dynamics becomes urgent the week a coalition shifts. A framework for mapping interests becomes essential the morning before a difficult conversation. The material here is meant to be available when it is needed, not only when a table of contents suggests it should appear.

The fourteen chapters follow a natural progression. Part I lays the conceptual foundation: why negotiation sits at the center of transformation, how resistance actually operates, and how stakeholder ecosystems shift over time. Part II introduces the core skills that practitioners use most directly: distinguishing interests from positions, mapping those interests, assessing leverage and alternatives, and using framing to shape how change is received. Part III moves into deeper territory, exploring the behavioral biases that drive irrational resistance, the game-theoretic dynamics that trap organizations in inefficient patterns, and the strategic choreography of multi-party negotiation. Part IV brings everything together into sustained practice: crisis response, adaptive leadership style, process design, and the work of building negotiation capability across teams and institutions.

A reader approaching the subject for the first time will find that this sequence builds naturally, each Part extending the ideas established before it. But few readers will come to this material without some prior experience, and many will arrive with a specific problem already in motion. For those readers, the chapters have been written to stand on their own well enough to be consulted out of sequence. Concepts introduced in earlier chapters are referenced where they appear later, so that the reader who enters at Chapter 10 is not left without context.

For readers facing a specific situation, the following entry points may be useful.

If you are preparing for a difficult alignment conversation and need to understand what the other party actually wants, Chapter 4 offers the interests-versus-positions framework, and Chapter 5 provides the mapping tools to structure your preparation.

If you are sensing quiet resistance but cannot identify its source, Chapter 2 provides a detailed anatomy of how resistance operates beneath the surface, including the behavioral signals that reveal hidden concerns.

If you need to assess your negotiating position before entering a high-stakes discussion, Chapter 6 introduces leverage, BATNA, and ZOPA as applied to internal organizational contexts.

If you are managing a complex initiative that requires alignment across multiple functions or regions, Chapter 10 addresses sequencing, coalition dynamics, and the choreography of multi-party negotiation.

If trust has broken down or a crisis has disrupted the program's momentum, Chapter 11 offers guidance on maintaining and rebuilding alignment under pressure.

If you are designing governance processes or incentive structures and want them to support rather than undermine alignment, Chapter 13 addresses how negotiation thinking can be embedded into organizational systems.

These are starting points rather than isolated destinations. Most readers will find themselves moving between chapters as their situation evolves, returning to foundational material after encountering a new challenge, or revisiting a practical framework once the conceptual context becomes clearer. The book is designed to support that kind of movement. It is meant to remain open and in active use throughout the arc of a transformation effort, not read once and set aside.

PART I
FOUNDATIONS

Chapter 1
Why Transformation Requires Negotiation

The program had everything it was supposed to have. Executive sponsorship from two members of the leadership team. A business case that had survived three rounds of scrutiny. A detailed implementation plan with workstreams, milestones, and a governance structure that looked, on paper, like it could absorb any reasonable disruption. The initiative was designed to consolidate procurement operations across four regions into a shared service model, and the projected savings were substantial enough to justify the complexity. When the program was formally launched at a leadership offsite in early March, the response in the room was unanimously supportive. Heads nodded. Questions were constructive. The sponsor closed the session by saying she felt confident that alignment was strong.

Six months later, the program had not failed in any dramatic or visible way. No one had openly opposed it. No faction had organized resistance. What had happened was subtler and, in many respects, more damaging. Regional teams had begun interpreting the shared service model differently. Two regions had started parallel workstreams that duplicated effort without coordination. A third had quietly delayed key decisions, citing the need for further analysis that never seemed to conclude. The procurement leads in each region continued to attend program meetings and report progress, but the substance behind those reports had grown thin. Commitments made in steering committees were not translating into action on the ground.

The program lead, a seasoned operations director who had managed large initiatives before, spent several weeks trying to diagnose the problem. She reviewed the plan. She examined the governance structure. She tested whether the business case still held. Everything checked out. It was only after a series of candid one-on-one conversations with regional stakeholders that the real picture emerged. The strategy was not the issue. The issue was that the conversations required to build genuine alignment across the regions had never happened with sufficient depth. People had agreed to the concept without agreeing on what it would actually mean for their teams, their processes, and their authority. The program had launched on the strength of surface consensus, and that surface had been eroding quietly from the start.

This pattern is more common than most organizations acknowledge. Programs stall not because their strategies are flawed but because the alignment they depend on was never as solid as it appeared. The conversations that produce durable agreement are different in character from the conversations that produce formal approval. They are slower, more granular, and more concerned with the specific interests that each group brings to the table. When those conversations are skipped or compressed, the result is a kind of organizational drift where stated commitment and actual behavior gradually diverge.

Transformation depends on negotiation, understood here as something quite different from the deal-making associated with contracts and counterparties. Building and sustaining agreement among groups whose interests differ, overlap, and keep shifting: that is the practice that provides architecture to a transformation. Without it, even the most carefully designed programs operate on borrowed alignment that weakens under pressure.

Transformation as a Continuous Condition

Traditional views of organizational change tend to assume a relatively stable pattern. A new strategy is defined, a program is launched, the organization adjusts, and a new equilibrium is reached. This image no longer reflects how most organizations experience change. Advances in technology, the entry of new competitors, evolving regulatory requirements, and shifting workforce expectations create an environment where new pressures arrive before earlier ones have fully settled. The intervals between major initiatives have compressed to the point where many organizations are running multiple transformation programs simultaneously, each competing for the same leadership attention, the same operational capacity, and the same willingness to absorb disruption.

Under these conditions, transformation is not experienced as an event with a beginning and an end. It becomes the backdrop against which everyday decisions are made. Teams are asked to adopt new tools while still learning the ones introduced the previous year. Managers are expected to maintain operational performance while also driving structural changes to how their functions operate. Priorities shift with each quarterly review, and the rationale for those shifts is not always communicated with the clarity or consistency that people need in order to adjust their own work. The cumulative effect is an environment where uncertainty is constant and where the capacity to absorb change becomes as important as the capacity to design it.

This continuity has significant implications for how alignment is built and maintained. When change was episodic, it was possible to secure agreement at the outset and rely on that agreement to hold through implementation. When change is continuous, initial agreement is only a starting point. The expectations placed on individuals and teams evolve as the program unfolds, as new information becomes available, and as the broader organizational context shifts. Their willingness to remain committed depends on whether they continue to understand the purpose of the change, whether they see fairness in how burdens and benefits are distributed, and whether they trust that their concerns will be acknowledged rather than set aside. These factors cannot be secured through a single announcement or a well-constructed launch event. They require ongoing conversations that connect strategic intent to the lived experience of the people who must carry the work forward.

This ongoing quality makes negotiation essential. A plan can be designed once. Alignment must be built and rebuilt continuously. The discipline required to sustain that alignment, to detect when it is weakening, to understand why, and to restore it before drift becomes dysfunction, is the discipline of negotiation applied to the internal life of the organization.

Negotiation as the Practice of Building Alignment

Negotiation plays a distinctive role in transformation work, yet most organizations fail to recognize it. They associate negotiation with external relationships: contracts, vendor agreements, partnerships, regulatory settlements. When the word appears in an internal context, it often carries a faintly political connotation, as though negotiating inside the organization were a sign of dysfunction rather than a sign of maturity. This association obscures the reality that every significant transformation depends on a series of internal agreements, most of which are never formalized but all of which shape whether the work moves forward or stalls.

What negotiation provides, when practiced with discipline, is a structured way to uncover what different groups require in order to support a new direction. Rather than aiming to settle disputes after they have escalated, negotiation shapes the early conditions under which cooperation becomes possible. Through careful conversation, leaders can test whether their assumptions about stakeholder readiness are accurate, clarify expectations that may have been left vague during the planning phase, and identify practical or emotional barriers that do not appear in formal planning documents.

In this sense, negotiation is a leadership practice concerned with alignment. It supports the construction of agreements that account for the pressures faced by various teams. It helps identify what must be adjusted in order for different groups to commit without feeling that their core interests have been compromised. It also provides a method for reshaping decisions when circumstances change, so that the organization does not lose momentum when new information comes to light or when the environment shifts in ways that the original plan did not anticipate.

When leaders engage with the real interests behind stated positions, they create space for honest discussion. Individuals are more willing to express concerns when those concerns will be treated seriously rather than dismissed as obstacles. That engagement prevents misunderstandings from hardening into refusal and opens alternatives that address the needs of multiple groups at once. The procurement program described at the opening of this chapter lacked this kind of engagement. The conversations that took place were transactional and confirmatory. They sought approval rather than understanding, and the result was alignment that looked solid in the conference room but dissolved in the hallways.

How Hidden Interests Shape Outcomes

Positions are often the most visible elements in organizational decision-making, yet they rarely reveal the full picture of what is driving behavior. A team may insist on maintaining local control over a process that the transformation seeks to centralize. A function may claim the need for additional resources before it can participate. A regional leader may question the timing of an initiative while expressing support for its goals. These positions are real, but they represent the surface layer of a deeper landscape.

Beneath each position lie interests that are more difficult to express and, in many organizational cultures, more difficult to acknowledge. A team insisting on local control may be protecting workload stability during an already demanding period. It may be concerned that centralization will expose performance gaps that have been managed quietly for years. It may fear that the people who understand the local context will lose influence to a central team that does not. These interests are not irrational, and they are not signs of bad faith. They are the natural concerns of people who are being asked to change something that has worked well enough and to accept uncertainty about what will replace it.

When hidden interests remain unidentified, decisions appear to stall for reasons that seem disconnected from the stated positions. Meetings cycle through the same discussions without producing new clarity. Support weakens, not because the strategy is flawed but because the concerns influencing behavior have never been surfaced or addressed. The program team grows frustrated with what it perceives as resistance, while the stakeholders grow frustrated with what they perceive as indifference to their realities.

Negotiation provides a pathway to uncover these interests by exploring the reasoning behind each position and by interpreting the signals that people give when they hesitate, become overly cautious, or push for procedural delays that serve no obvious purpose. Once identified, these interests can be addressed in ways that produce more stable cooperation. Adjustments to timelines, changes in role definitions, targeted support for specific teams, or clearer articulation of long-term benefits often emerge from these conversations. This framework, the distinction between positions and interests, is central to the approach developed throughout this book and will be explored in full depth in Chapter 4. For the present purpose, it is enough to recognize that the visible landscape of a transformation is only the surface, and that the forces shaping its trajectory operate largely beneath that surface.

Negotiation Across the Layers of a Transformation Program

The complexity of modern transformation requires negotiation to operate at several interconnected levels. The nature of the conversations changes at each level, as do the interests at stake and the pressures that shape behavior.

At the executive layer, leaders must reconcile competing priorities across functions or regions. Each leader balances organizational goals with the interests of their own teams and the realities of their own operational constraints. Negotiation at this level clarifies what each area requires in order to move forward without placing disproportionate burden on others. It also surfaces the strategic trade-offs that formal planning often smooths over, revealing where genuine disagreement exists about direction, pace, or resource allocation.

At the program layer, cross-functional groups must determine how timelines, resources, and responsibilities will be shared. Differences in capacity, competing operational demands, and varying interpretations of risk all influence these discussions. Negotiation helps ensure that commitments made at this level are credible and that the program structure supports collaboration rather than constraining it. When program-level agreements are built on genuine understanding of what each function can deliver, they hold. When they are built on optimistic assumptions, they fracture under the first serious pressure.

At the team layer, negotiation shapes how the transformation is interpreted in the context of real, daily work. New processes require changes in behavior and adjustments in how work is coordinated. Concerns about workload, skill requirements, or the loss of established routines surface most acutely here. Engaging with these concerns directly strengthens adoption and reduces the likelihood of the quiet withdrawal that erodes implementation from within.

Even at the individual level, negotiation plays a role that is easy to overlook. Employees facing changes in their daily responsibilities must reconcile their own expectations with the demands of the new environment. When they feel heard and supported, they contribute with greater confidence and willingness to experiment. When they feel dismissed or uninformed, they retreat into familiar patterns and contribute the minimum required.

The following table summarizes how negotiation operates across these four layers, including the typical sources of tension at each level and what effective negotiation makes possible.

Table 1.

The Multi-Layer Architecture of Negotiation in Transformation Programs

Layer	Core Purpose of Negotiation	Typical Sources of Tension	What Effective Negotiation Enables
Executive Layer	Reconcile competing priorities across functions or regions while preserving enterprise coherence.	Balancing organizational goals with local interests; concerns about uneven burden; strategic ambiguity during shifting conditions.	Clear understanding of what each area needs in order to commit; fair distribution of responsibilities; alignment that can withstand pressure.
Program Layer	Determine how timelines, resources, and responsibilities will be shared across cross-functional groups.	Differences in capacity, workload, operational rhythms, and interpretations of risk; competing workstreams.	Credible commitments; program structures that support collaboration rather than constraining it; early detection of feasibility issues.
Team Layer	Shape the local interpretation of the transformation and clarify what the change means in real work.	Concerns about workload, skill gaps, process changes, loss of autonomy, and unclear expectations.	Stronger adoption; reduced passive resistance; practical adjustments that reflect team realities; smoother coordination.
Individual Layer	Help employees reconcile personal expectations with new responsibilities or shifting workflows.	Uncertainty about roles, fear of exposure, overload, limited information, or loss of familiarity.	Increased confidence; willingness to experiment with new behaviors; reduced withdrawal into old routines; more consistent engagement.

Across all four layers, negotiation provides coherence. It allows different groups to connect their interests with the broader direction of the organization. It creates conditions where cooperation becomes a natural response rather than a compliance exercise, and where shared commitment can be maintained even when challenges intensify. The architecture of a transformation is not found in its project plan or its governance charter. It is found in the quality of the agreements that hold the work together at every level, and in the ongoing conversations that keep those agreements alive.

Transformation becomes more durable when negotiation is treated as an ongoing practice rather than an occasional intervention reserved for moments of visible conflict. It strengthens the relationships and agreements that sustain the work over time, and it equips leaders to interpret signals that might otherwise be missed. What tests those agreements most consistently is not strategic failure or inadequate resources. It is resistance, in forms that are often quieter and more systemic than the word suggests.

Chapter 2
The Anatomy of Resistance

The operations team had been among the first to endorse the new workflow management platform. Their director spoke positively about it during the steering committee, volunteered his team for the second wave of onboarding, and assigned a capable project coordinator to serve as the team's liaison with the implementation group. For the first several weeks, everything appeared to be on track. Status updates were submitted on time. The coordinator attended every working session. When the program lead reviewed the dashboard at the end of the first month, the operations team showed green across every metric that measured participation.

It was the quality of the participation that told a different story. Tasks were being completed in the narrowest possible sense. Data migration forms were submitted but with gaps that required rework. Testing scenarios were marked as done but had been run only partially. Questions that would normally surface during a hands-on adoption process were not being raised, and when the implementation team offered additional support, the response was polite but vague. Follow-up actions from meetings were acknowledged but not acted upon with any urgency. Nothing was refused. Nothing was delayed in a way that could be flagged as non-compliance. But nothing was moving with the kind of engagement that a genuine adoption requires.

The program lead initially attributed the pattern to workload. The operations team was managing a heavy quarter-end cycle, and it seemed reasonable that their attention was divided. It was only after an informal conversation with the project coordinator, over coffee and away from any formal setting, that a clearer picture emerged. The coordinator, who trusted the program lead enough to speak candidly, explained that several senior members of the team were concerned about what the new platform would reveal. The existing workflow system was familiar, and its limitations were well understood. More importantly, those limitations had allowed the team to manage certain inefficiencies quietly, compensating through institutional knowledge and informal workarounds that had developed over years. The new platform, with its transparency and standardized reporting, threatened to make those workarounds visible. The concern was not about the technology. It was about exposure.

The team had not resisted the initiative in any way that could be identified through normal project governance. There was no opposition to document, no escalation to manage. What had happened was quieter and, for that reason, more difficult to address. The team had calculated, without ever discussing it explicitly, that the safest response was to participate just enough to avoid scrutiny while withholding the deeper engagement that would make the new system genuinely operational. The resistance was real, but it had taken a form that was almost invisible from the outside.

Resistance inside transformation programs is not a character flaw or an expression of defiance. It is a systemic response to uncertainty, produced by the interaction of structural pressures, psychological needs, and cultural norms. Understanding its anatomy is essential for any leader who wants to build alignment that holds, because resistance that is misread is resistance that compounds.

How Resistance Operates as a System

Leaders often interpret resistance through an individual lens. A stakeholder is described as "resistant" in the same way they might be described as skeptical or cautious, as though resistance were a personal characteristic rather than an organizational phenomenon. This framing is understandable but misleading. It directs attention toward the individual and away from the conditions that produced the behavior, and it leads to interventions, typically persuasion or escalation, that address symptoms rather than causes.

In transformation contexts, resistance functions more like a systemic response to disruption. Individuals and groups seek stability in the structures that have supported them: established roles, familiar processes, trusted relationships, and predictable patterns of authority. When these anchors are disrupted, protective behaviors emerge. Teams slow their pace. Decision-making becomes more cautious. People revert to familiar routines even when those routines have been formally replaced. None of these behaviors necessarily originate in personal opposition to the change. They arise from the interaction of structural pressures that shape how work is distributed, psychological needs that favor predictability and competence, and cultural norms that influence how disagreement and uncertainty are expressed.

Organizational history reinforces these patterns in ways that are easy to underestimate. Past initiatives that failed to deliver their promised benefits leave lasting impressions, particularly on the teams that absorbed the heaviest costs. Functions that struggled to meet expectations during earlier transformations carry forward a wariness that shapes how they approach new proposals. Groups that once invested heavily in a change only to see it reversed or abandoned develop a rational skepticism toward the next program that asks for their commitment. These memories become part of the organizational fabric. They travel through informal conversations, influence how new information is interpreted, and shape behavior long before any formal expression of resistance appears.

Recognizing the systemic nature of resistance changes the way leaders respond to it. The focus shifts from persuading individuals to understanding the conditions that make protective behavior rational. Resistance becomes information rather than obstruction: a signal about where alignment is incomplete and where the underlying interests have not yet been addressed.

What the Surface Shows and What It Conceals

The visible expressions of resistance are familiar to anyone who has led or participated in a transformation program. Questions about timelines. Concerns about resource availability. Requests for additional analysis before commitments are made. Cautious or partial endorsements that stop short of full engagement. These surface expressions are real, and they deserve to be taken seriously. They reflect the practical pressures of ongoing work and the legitimate demands of the initiative. But they also tend to underrepresent the real sources of hesitation.

Hidden drivers of resistance are often more instructive than the visible ones. Individuals may fear that the change will expose gaps in capability that they have managed to keep contained. They may sense that the risks of the initiative fall disproportionately on their team while the benefits accrue elsewhere. They may recall previous transformations that demanded heavy sacrifices without delivering what was promised. They may worry about losing influence over decisions that matter to their professional identity or their standing within the organization. Such concerns do not usually appear in direct language. Instead, they take the form of cautious commitments, repeated requests for reassurance, reluctance to move beyond preliminary tasks, or the kind of minimal compliance that the operations team in the opening example demonstrated.

The relationship between surface expressions and hidden drivers is not one of deception. Most people do not deliberately conceal their concerns. They may not have fully articulated those concerns to themselves, or they may judge, correctly in many organizational cultures, that expressing deeper fears openly would be seen as weakness or as insufficient commitment to the program. The surface layer is what feels safe to say. The hidden layer is what actually shapes behavior.

Understanding this distinction is essential because the two layers call for different responses. Surface concerns can often be addressed through adjustments to plans, timelines, or resource allocation. Hidden drivers require a different kind of engagement: conversations that create enough trust for the real concerns to emerge, and responses that demonstrate those concerns are being taken seriously rather than managed or dismissed.

Table 2.

Surface Expressions and Hidden Drivers of Resistance

Dimension	What It Looks Like	Underlying Meaning	Implications for Transformation
Surface Expressions	Questions about timelines, resource constraints, feasibility, or clarity; cautious or partial commitments.	Reflect the practical pressures of ongoing work and the visible demands of the initiative.	Provide early signals but often underrepresent the real sources of hesitation; should prompt deeper inquiry.
Hidden Drivers	Reluctance to move beyond preliminary tasks; repeated requests for reassurance; subtle delays in decision-making.	Concerns about capability gaps, loss of influence, uneven distribution of risk, or memories of past failed transformations.	Shape long-term cooperation more strongly than surface statements; require careful exploration to prevent misalignment from deepening.
Narrative Behind Resistance	Interpretations formed through personal experience, group expectations, informal signals, and organizational history.	Influence how individuals judge fairness, safety, and credibility.	Determine whether agreement becomes stable commitment or symbolic compliance.

Structural, Psychological, and Cultural Friction

Resistance does not arise from a single source. It is produced by the overlap of three distinct types of friction, each of which operates through different mechanisms and requires different responses.

Structural friction emerges from the design of the organization itself. When responsibilities are distributed across different functions or regions, alignment demands shared interpretation, shared timing, and a shared willingness to adjust priorities. Processes that were built to maintain consistency and control can become obstacles when adaptation is needed quickly. Governance bodies designed for steady-state operations may lack the flexibility to reconcile decisions that affect multiple groups simultaneously. Reporting lines create incentives that do not always align with the transformation's requirements. These structural patterns make alignment difficult even when every party involved genuinely supports the intention of the change. The friction is not personal. It is architectural.

Psychological friction adds a different kind of complexity. Individuals rely on familiar routines to manage the cognitive demands of their work. When those routines are disrupted, ambiguity increases the mental effort required to make even routine decisions. Concerns about performance become more acute. Small misunderstandings feel amplified because the usual interpretive frameworks no longer apply. The result is often a preference for incremental movement rather than decisive shifts, not because people lack commitment but because the cognitive demands of changing established habits while maintaining the quality of ongoing work are genuinely heavy. This tendency is a natural response to overload, and treating it as reluctance misses the point entirely.

Cultural friction operates more quietly but just as persistently. Organizations develop shared expectations about how disagreement should be expressed, how authority should be interpreted, and how risk should be managed. In some cultures, disagreement emerges openly and is treated as a healthy part of decision-making. In others, disagreement is softened through partial endorsement, deferred action, or silence that is easily mistaken for consent. Organizational history plays an influential role here as well. If previous changes resulted in uneven outcomes, skepticism becomes widespread regardless of the current program's merits. If the culture prizes autonomy, central guidance may be perceived as intrusive. If the culture values caution, requests for speed will be met with hesitation even when the business case is compelling. These cultural forces shape how messages are received and how decisions are carried forward long after formal approval has been granted.

Table 3.

Structural, Psychological, and Cultural Friction Patterns

Friction Type	How It Manifests in Daily Work	Underlying Mechanisms	Impact on Transformation
Structural Friction	Misaligned timelines across functions, slow coordination between regions, rigid processes that resist adaptation, governance bodies unable to reconcile cross-functional trade-offs.	Organizational design distributes authority, responsibility, and incentives unevenly; processes optimized for stability struggle under conditions requiring flexibility.	Alignment becomes difficult even when intentions are shared; cooperation slows as teams protect their own operational constraints.
Psychological Friction	Preference for incremental changes, reluctance to commit fully, heightened need for reassurance, amplified reactions to small misunderstandings.	Increased cognitive load from ambiguity; disrupted routines deprive individuals of familiar anchors, concerns about competence, performance, and exposure intensify under uncertainty.	Adoption decelerates not due to opposition but due to cognitive strain; individuals retreat to familiar behaviors unless expectations and support are clarified.
Cultural Friction	Indirect expression of disagreement, cautious endorsement, reliance on informal channels, uneven enthusiasm across regions or functions.	Shared norms around authority, risk, and communication shape how people interpret expectations; historical memories influence trust and credibility; values such as autonomy or caution drive local interpretations.	Messages are received unevenly across the organization; formal approval may not translate into practical commitment; hidden skepticism persists even in environments that appear aligned on the surface.

The interaction between these three types of friction is what makes resistance so difficult to diagnose and so easy to misjudge. A team that appears to be dragging its feet may be experiencing all three simultaneously: a governance structure that does not give them clear authority to act, a cognitive burden that makes the new process feel overwhelming, and a cultural norm that discourages them from saying so directly. Addressing only one of these forces while the others remain active will produce limited results. Effective response requires seeing the full picture.

Competing Priorities and the Weight of Cognitive Overload

Transformation does not arrive into an empty calendar. It lands on top of ongoing responsibilities, quarterly targets, existing projects, and the accumulated obligations of organizational life. The additional demands placed on teams must coexist with everything that was already there, and the people absorbing those demands must make daily judgments about what deserves immediate attention and what can be deferred.

When priorities compete, individuals fall back on what is familiar and what feels manageable. This is not a failure of commitment. It is a rational response to the reality that human attention is finite and that the costs of neglecting existing responsibilities are often more immediate and more visible than the costs of slowing a transformation. The transformation asks people to invest in an uncertain future. Their existing work asks them to perform in a measured and accountable present. When the two compete, the present usually wins.

Cognitive overload compounds this effect. Transformations introduce new vocabulary, unfamiliar processes, revised reporting structures, and increased interdependence across teams. Individuals must process more information than usual while continuing to perform at the standard expected of them. As the cognitive burden increases, people gravitate toward clarity and away from ambiguity. They may postpone decisions until they feel better equipped to evaluate the options. They may avoid raising questions that could reveal uncertainty or invite additional complexity. These behaviors reduce the pace of adoption and undermine the coherence that the transformation requires, but they are not signs of opposition. They are signs of a system under strain.

Three Patterns That Rarely Announce Themselves

Resistance in its most consequential forms tends to be quiet. The three patterns that do the most damage to transformation programs are also the three that are hardest to detect through conventional project governance.

Quiet refusal is the pattern illustrated by the operations team at the start of this chapter. Individuals and groups voice support publicly while slowing their actual engagement. Tasks remain partially completed. Follow-up actions are acknowledged but not prioritized. Meetings conclude with apparent agreement but produce little practical movement. The hallmark of quiet refusal is that it blends seamlessly into the normal rhythm of organizational life. Every individual action, taken in isolation, appears reasonable. Only the cumulative pattern reveals the resistance, and that pattern is visible only to someone paying close attention.

Symbolic agreement takes a different form. Here, stakeholders endorse a decision in principle while withholding full commitment to its specific implications. A regional leader might support the strategy while quietly insisting that their region's implementation be delayed. A functional head might agree to the new operating model while retaining parallel processes that effectively preserve the status quo. Symbolic agreement provides temporary stability because it looks like alignment. The program moves forward. Reports are positive. But the underlying commitment is shallow, and it erodes quickly the first time the agreement is tested by a concrete demand that requires genuine change. Consider the experience of a compliance transformation where every business unit signed off on the new framework during the design phase but three of the five units continued to operate under their legacy procedures for months after go-live, treating the formal sign-off as the end of their obligation rather than the beginning.

Passive drift is perhaps the most insidious of the three because it has no identifiable starting point. Early enthusiasm gradually dissolves into routine execution. Goals that once felt urgent become abstract. Teams continue to perform the tasks assigned to them but lose their connection to the larger purpose of the change. The energy that characterized the launch phase dissipates without any single event to explain the shift. Passive drift is the cumulative result of unresolved concerns, competing priorities, unclear incentives, and the natural tendency of organizational attention to migrate toward whatever feels most pressing in the moment. It can persist for months, even years, particularly in organizations that are accustomed to cycles of ambitious initiatives followed by uneven implementation.

Recognizing Misalignment Before It Hardens

These patterns share one important feature: they are most responsive to intervention when they are still forming. Once quiet refusal becomes established behavior, once symbolic agreement has been tested and found to carry no consequences, once passive drift has become the team's default mode, reversing the pattern requires significantly more effort than preventing it would have required. Early detection is not merely useful. It is one of the most valuable capabilities a transformation leader can develop.

Several indicators appear before resistance becomes fully visible. Repeated reinterpretation of the same directive suggests that teams do not share a common understanding of what the change actually requires. When different groups describe the same initiative in meaningfully different terms, the issue is not communication failure in any simple sense. It is a sign that people are interpreting the change through the lens of their own concerns, and that those concerns have not been adequately surfaced or addressed.

Slowed decision-making, particularly when the reasons offered remain vague or circular, signals that hesitations are forming beneath the surface. When approval processes take longer than expected and the explanations do not point to any specific obstacle, the delay itself is the message. Something is unresolved, and the individuals involved may not yet have the language or the trust to articulate what it is.

Growing reliance on procedural language is another telling sign. When stakeholders begin referencing policy, precedent, or established process more frequently than the goals of the transformation, they are anchoring themselves to the familiar as a way of managing uncertainty. This is not obstruction. It is a search for solid ground in an environment that feels unstable.

Inconsistent narratives across functions or regions reveal misalignment in its most visible early form. When the finance team describes the transformation as primarily a cost exercise while the technology team describes it as a capability upgrade and the operations team describes it as an imposition on their workflow, the divergence reflects genuine differences in how the initiative is being experienced. These differences, left unaddressed, will widen over time and produce the kind of fragmented implementation that undermines the program's coherence.

A general atmosphere of caution, a sense that people are waiting for clarity before committing, is perhaps the most diffuse indicator but also one of the most reliable. When the prevailing posture shifts from engagement to observation, something in the alignment has weakened. The cause may not yet be identifiable, but the signal itself should prompt inquiry.

Table 4

Early Indicators of Misalignment in Transformation

Indicator	What It Looks Like	What It Suggests Beneath the Surface	Implications for the Transformation
Repeated Reinterpretation of the Same Directive	Teams define or describe the same instruction in different ways; explanations drift over time.	Lack of shared understanding; unresolved concerns influencing interpretation; inconsistent framing across groups.	Alignment weakens before resistance becomes visible; clarity must be restored to prevent long-term divergence.
Slowed Decision-Making with Vague Justifications	Approvals take longer, follow-up steps remain unclear, and reasons for delay feel incomplete or circular.	Emerging hesitation; fear of making the wrong commitment; early signs of hidden doubts or perceived risks.	Momentum decreases; leadership intervention is needed to surface concerns before positions harden.
Growing Reliance on Procedural Language	Stakeholders reference policy, process, or precedent rather than engaging with new expectations.	Desire for safety and familiarity; anchoring to established norms due to uncertainty or cognitive load.	Innovation stalls as teams retreat into routine; conversations must shift toward the intent and rationale behind the change.
Inconsistent Narratives Across Functions or Regions	Different groups describe the purpose, urgency, or expected outcomes of the transformation in incompatible ways.	Misalignment in interpretation, cultural filters, or structural pressures shaping local perspectives.	Fragmentation increases; unified communication and targeted engagement become essential.
General Sense of Caution or "Waiting for Clarity"	Teams slow action while stating support, or defer commitments until conditions feel more settled.	Unresolved interests, fear of uneven burden, or insufficient trust that concerns will be heard.	Signals opportunity for early intervention; engagement should focus on understanding rather than persuasion.

These indicators are often subtle enough to be dismissed as routine noise. In a busy organization managing multiple priorities, slowed decisions and cautious language may look like nothing more than a crowded agenda. The discipline required is to recognize that these signals, when they cluster together or persist across multiple groups, carry meaning that deserves investigation. The transformation leader who pays attention to these early patterns and responds with inquiry rather than escalation gains something that is difficult to recover once it is lost: the opportunity to address misalignment while it is still fluid, before it crystallizes into the fixed positions and entrenched behaviors that make later negotiation far more difficult.

Understanding resistance in this way reframes the entire relationship between a transformation program and the people it depends on. Resistance is not a problem to be solved through better messaging or stronger mandates. It is information about where the alignment needs work, where interests remain unaddressed, and where the conditions for cooperation have not yet been fully established. The terrain where that cooperation must be built is the stakeholder ecosystem, with its informal power structures, shifting coalitions, and cultural filters that shape how every negotiation unfolds.

Chapter 3
Stakeholder Ecosystems: Power, Coalitions, and Shifting Ground

When the enterprise resource planning program was approved in January, one of its most visible supporters was the head of supply chain operations for the Northern European region. He had spoken favorably about the initiative during the design phase, contributed his team's requirements to the scoping process, and told the program director privately that he considered the modernization overdue. His support mattered. He was well respected across the organization, not only within his own function but among peers in finance, commercial, and technology who valued his judgment and his track record of pragmatic leadership. If the program had a stakeholder map in January, his name would have appeared firmly in the supporter column.

By April, his position had changed. Not dramatically, and not through any public statement. He had simply grown quieter. His attendance at steering committee meetings became intermittent. When he did attend, his contributions shifted from advocacy to procedural questions about sequencing and resource allocation. The program team noticed the change in tone but attributed it to the pressures of a difficult first quarter. It was not until a working session in late April, when two of his direct reports raised concerns about the implementation timeline that closely echoed each other's language, that the program director began to suspect that something more deliberate was at work.

What had happened was not complicated, but it was invisible to anyone relying on formal channels. Over the course of February and March, the supply chain head had been in regular conversation with counterparts in two other regions who were further along in their own assessment of what the new system would require. Those conversations revealed that the workload implications of the migration were substantially heavier than the formal briefings had indicated, particularly for teams that managed complex supplier networks across multiple regulatory environments. The concern was not abstract. It was specific: his team would need to maintain full operational performance during a transition period that now appeared longer and more resource-intensive than originally presented. He had raised this with the program team once, received a reassuring but general response, and concluded that the gap between the program's assumptions and his team's reality was not being taken seriously.

His shift from supporter to skeptic was consequential not only because of his own position but because of the network effects it produced. Two other regional heads, both of whom had been cautiously supportive, began to recalibrate their own positions after informal conversations with him. A small coalition of middle managers across the three regions, connected through a long-standing operational community of practice, started sharing concerns about the implementation timeline through their own channels. By the time the program team recognized that alignment had weakened, the shift was no longer confined to one individual. It had traveled through relationships that no org chart depicted and no governance structure monitored.

Stakeholders are not static entries on a planning document. They are participants in dynamic networks whose positions evolve continuously, shaped by informal relationships, shifting pressures, cultural context, and the daily experience of organizational life. How influence travels through that ecosystem, how coalitions form and reform, how to read the signals it sends: understanding these dynamics is foundational to the negotiation work this book develops.

Why Static Stakeholder Lists Fail

Stakeholder identification is one of the earliest activities in most transformation programs, and it is typically treated as a discrete task. Names are gathered, often through a combination of organizational charts and input from senior sponsors. Roles are assigned. Influence levels are estimated based on title, function, and proximity to decision-making authority. The resulting list or matrix provides initial clarity about who matters and how much attention each person or group should receive. As a starting exercise, this is reasonable. As a lasting representation of the stakeholder landscape, it is dangerously incomplete.

The fundamental problem with static stakeholder analysis is that it treats positions as fixed properties of individuals rather than as responses to evolving conditions. A manager who appears supportive during the design phase may become hesitant once the implications for her team become concrete. A department head who seemed neutral during planning may adopt a more active stance, either supportive or resistant, once he observes how other groups are responding and what precedents are being set. A senior leader who was genuinely enthusiastic at launch may quietly disengage once competing priorities absorb her attention and the transformation no longer feels like her most pressing concern.

These shifts occur because stakeholders are embedded in networks rather than occupying isolated positions. Their decisions reflect pressures from colleagues, concerns from their direct reports, expectations from senior leadership, and the cultural norms that influence how risk and commitment are interpreted within their part of the organization. A list cannot represent this complexity. It captures a snapshot of where people stood at one moment in time, and that snapshot begins to degrade the day it is created. Only by understanding stakeholders as participants in a living system can leaders anticipate how alignment will change, where new engagement is needed, and which relationships carry influence that no org chart will ever show.

Informal Power and the Influencers Who Never Appear on Lists

Formal authority is the most visible source of influence inside organizations, and it is often the only source that stakeholder analysis accounts for. A vice president's support is noted because her title implies decision-making power. A director's skepticism is flagged because his position in the hierarchy suggests he could slow implementation. These assessments are not wrong, but they are incomplete in ways that matter enormously during transformation.

In most organizations, the individuals who shape how a change is received are not always the ones whose names appear at the top of the relevant reporting lines. A technical expert whose judgment is widely trusted can determine whether a new system is adopted with genuine engagement or with the minimum compliance that quietly ensures its failure. A long-tenured operations manager with deep relationships across multiple teams can influence peer behavior in ways that no formal communication plan can replicate. An executive assistant who controls access to a senior leader's calendar and attention can accelerate or delay critical conversations without anyone recognizing her role in the outcome. These individuals rarely appear on stakeholder matrices, yet their impact on transformation outcomes is often profound.

Identifying hidden influencers requires a different kind of inquiry than the one that produces a standard stakeholder list. It means asking not only "Who has authority over this decision?" but also "Whose opinion do people seek before forming their own? Who do teams turn to when they are uncertain about how to interpret a new directive? Whose early adoption would signal to others that the change is credible and safe?" These questions point toward a map of actual influence that may differ significantly from the map of formal authority. Both maps matter. But during transformation, when formal commitments must translate into discretionary effort and genuine behavioral change, the informal map often matters more.

Coalition behavior follows a similar logic. Coalitions inside organizations do not typically form through deliberate coordination. They emerge from shared concerns, common experiences, or the natural clustering of people who face similar pressures and communicate regularly enough to recognize that they share a perspective. The three regional heads in the opening example did not decide to form an opposition bloc. They arrived at similar conclusions through parallel experiences and reinforced each other's interpretation through conversations that occurred naturally within their existing professional relationships.

This organic quality makes coalitions both powerful and difficult to see from the outside. A program team monitoring formal governance channels may detect no sign that a coalition is forming until its effects become visible in coordinated behavior, aligned talking points, or a synchronized withdrawal of engagement. Understanding coalition logic means recognizing that shared concerns will find each other, that informal communication networks are the channels through which alignment and misalignment both travel, and that the formation of a skeptical coalition is not an act of sabotage. It is the natural response of professionals who are processing the same information through the same set of concerns.

How Geography, Function, and Culture Filter Every Message

Stakeholder interpretation is shaped not only by individual interests and informal networks but also by the structural and cultural filters through which different groups process organizational priorities. These filters are not biases in the pejorative sense. They are the natural consequence of occupying different positions within a complex system, and they mean that the same message, delivered with the same words and the same intent, will be received differently depending on where the listener sits.

Geographic distance introduces the most obvious filter. A decision made at headquarters that feels reasonable within the context of the home market may impose unexpected burden on a team operating in a different regulatory environment, managing different customer expectations, or working within cultural norms that do not map neatly onto the assumptions embedded in the program design. Time zones compress the windows available for real-time collaboration. Communication rhythms differ: some regions expect frequent, informal updates while others operate on longer cycles with more formal touchpoints. Local resource constraints may make a global timeline unrealistic even when the local team fully supports the initiative's goals. These geographic realities are well known in principle but chronically underweighted in practice, partly because the people designing transformation programs tend to be located at or near the center and partly because the effort required to genuinely adapt for local conditions is substantial.

Functional filters operate with equal force. Finance teams evaluate transformation through the lens of cost control, risk mitigation, and predictable returns. Technology teams focus on system integrity, scalability, and technical debt. Operations teams prioritize continuity, throughput, and the reliability of established processes. Commercial teams are concerned with customer impact, market timing, and competitive positioning. Risk and compliance functions look for regulatory exposure and governance adequacy. Each of these perspectives is valid, and each reflects the professional incentives and stability needs of the function. But they create genuine differences in how urgency is assessed, how risks are weighted, and how trade-offs are evaluated. A program that appears urgent to the commercial team may feel premature to operations. A solution that satisfies the technology team's requirements may introduce complexity that finance considers unjustified. These functional differences produce misalignment not because anyone is acting in bad faith but because the filters are genuinely different.

Cultural filters are perhaps the most consequential and the hardest to read from outside. Some organizational cultures encourage open questioning and treat visible disagreement as a sign of engagement. In these environments, resistance is relatively easy to detect because it announces itself. Other cultures promote quiet alignment even when concerns remain unresolved. Disagreement is expressed through delay, through partial endorsement, through the careful withholding of the discretionary effort that distinguishes genuine adoption from surface compliance. In these cultures, the absence of overt opposition is a poor indicator of alignment, and the program team that takes silence as consent may be surprised when implementation reveals the depth of the unspoken concerns. History compounds the effect. In organizations where previous transformations delivered unevenly on their promises, the cultural default tends toward skepticism regardless of the current program's merits. Where the culture values autonomy, central direction may feel like encroachment. Where the culture rewards caution, speed will be perceived as recklessness.

Effective stakeholder engagement cannot rely on a single message delivered uniformly across the organization. The message must be interpreted through each of these filters, and the engagement must be adapted to reflect the reality that different groups are not merely hearing the message differently but experiencing the transformation differently.

What Happens When Pressure Reveals the Fault Lines

Stakeholder ecosystems do not remain stable under pressure. When deadlines tighten, when early assumptions prove unrealistic, when a pilot produces results that are ambiguous or disappointing, the ecosystem responds in ways that reveal underlying tensions that may have been invisible during calmer periods.

Pressure amplifies the interests at stake. As uncertainty increases, people become more attentive to the workload implications of the change, to potential losses of autonomy or influence, and to the distribution of risk across groups. Stakeholders who remained quiet during the planning phase become more vocal as the costs of participation become clearer. Supporters who offered conditional endorsement begin to test whether the conditions they assumed would be met are actually being honored. The boundaries between supporters, skeptics, and the undecided become more fluid. A coalition that formed around cautious neutrality may shift toward active skepticism if unresolved concerns accumulate without acknowledgment. Another may increase its support if early results demonstrate that the transformation is delivering on its commitments or if the program team's response to problems builds confidence that difficulties will be managed fairly.

These shifts are not random. They follow patterns that become readable once leaders understand what to look for. A change in tone from a previously supportive stakeholder is often the first signal. So is an increase in the frequency or specificity of questions about implementation details, particularly when those questions come from individuals who had previously been content with high-level briefings. When stakeholders begin requesting bilateral conversations rather than engaging through formal channels, it usually indicates that their concerns have become specific enough to require a different kind of discussion. When previously separate groups begin using similar language to describe their hesitations, it suggests that informal communication has produced a shared interpretation that the program team should understand.

Leaders who recognize these shifts early gain a significant advantage. The period during which positions are forming but not yet fixed is the period of maximum opportunity for negotiation. Engaging stakeholders while their concerns are still evolving, before those concerns have crystallized into firm positions or been reinforced by coalition consensus, allows for the kind of flexible, interest-based conversation that produces durable alignment. Once positions harden, the negotiation becomes more constrained and the cost of adjustment rises for everyone involved.

Mapping the Ecosystem: Supporters, Skeptics, and the Undecided

Effective stakeholder mapping goes beyond the binary categories that most planning frameworks employ. Labeling someone as a "supporter" or a "blocker" provides the illusion of clarity while obscuring the conditions that actually determine behavior. A more useful approach distinguishes not only between categories but within them, recognizing that each category contains significant variation and that the most important information often lies in the conditions under which movement is likely.

Supporters, for example, are not a uniform group. Some offer strong, substantive support rooted in genuine alignment between the transformation's goals and their own interests. Others offer conditional support that depends on specific assurances being honored: a commitment to a particular timeline, a guarantee that resources will be provided, or an understanding that certain aspects of their operation will be protected during the transition. Still others offer symbolic support, endorsing the initiative publicly while privately reserving judgment about whether they will invest the effort required to make it succeed within their area of responsibility. Understanding which type of support a given stakeholder is providing matters because the implications for engagement are entirely different. Strong supporters can be mobilized as advocates. Conditional supporters need their conditions monitored and honored. Symbolic supporters need to be drawn into deeper engagement before their surface endorsement is tested by real demands.

Skeptics deserve similar differentiation. Some skepticism is practical, rooted in legitimate concerns about capacity, capability, or timing that reflect real constraints rather than resistance to change. Some is structural, arising from organizational design that creates misaligned incentives or conflicting priorities. Some is experiential, shaped by memories of past programs that failed to deliver or that imposed heavy costs on the skeptic's team. These different roots call for different responses. Practical skepticism is often the easiest to address because the concerns are specific and testable. Structural skepticism may require changes to governance or incentive design that go beyond the program team's immediate authority. Experiential skepticism requires the most patience because it will only shift in response to demonstrated evidence that this program operates differently from the ones that created the skepticism in the first place.

The undecided are frequently the most consequential group and the one that receives the least deliberate attention. These stakeholders are watching. They are observing how early adopters are treated, whether early concerns are addressed or dismissed, whether the program's promises hold up against initial reality, and how the power dynamics around the transformation evolve. Their interpretation of these early signals often determines whether the program builds the broad-based momentum it needs or stalls at the level of support it secured at launch. Engaging the undecided does not require persuasion so much as it requires providing them with the information, the early evidence, and the sense of fair treatment that allows them to conclude, on their own terms, that engagement is worthwhile.

Table 5.

Mapping Supporters, Skeptics, and the Undecided

Stakeholder Category	How They Present Themselves	Underlying Dynamics	Implications for Engagement
Supporters	Express endorsement of the initiative; may signal enthusiasm or willingness to participate in early activities.	Support may be strong, conditional, or symbolic. Some support because the strategy aligns with their interests; others support publicly while reserving judgment privately.	Clarify whether support is substantive or performative; reinforce their role in shaping momentum; monitor for shifts if new burdens emerge.
Skeptics	Raise concerns related to feasibility, workload, timing, capability, or past experiences with similar changes.	Skepticism may arise from practical constraints, structural pressures, cultural expectations, or organizational memory of previous failures.	Engage to understand the basis of their hesitation; differentiate between legitimate constraints and protective behavior; address concerns before they harden.
Undecided Stakeholders	Display caution or limited engagement; wait for early signals before committing; seek reassurance from peers or influential figures.	Their views are shaped by local conditions, informal networks, and early perceptions of fairness, feasibility, and leadership credibility.	Provide clarity and early wins; monitor interpretation patterns; intervene quickly if their narrative begins drifting away from the program's intent.
Cross-Cutting Consideration: Degree of Certainty	Shifts in tone, engagement level, or sentiment appear over time.	Stakeholder positions evolve as pressure, visibility, and expectations change.	Treat mapping as a living exercise; update regularly to reflect movement across categories.
Cross-Cutting Consideration: Influence Networks	Formal authority may not predict actual influence.	Informal networks shape sentiment and can accelerate or undermine alignment.	Identify hidden influencers; design engagement strategies that reflect both formal and informal pathways.

Keeping the Map Alive

A stakeholder map is only as valuable as its currency. The most common failure in stakeholder analysis is not that the initial map is poorly constructed but that it is treated as a finished product rather than as a working tool that requires regular revision. Organizations invest significant effort in the initial mapping exercise, produce a document that represents the landscape at one point in time, and then reference that document for months afterward without updating it. By the time the map is consulted during a critical decision, it may bear little resemblance to the reality it was meant to represent.

Several specific pitfalls recur with enough frequency to deserve attention. The first is confusing titles with influence. An individual's position in the hierarchy is a useful starting point but an unreliable predictor of how much their support or opposition will affect outcomes. The second is treating all categories as equally stable. Supporters can shift. Skeptics can be won over. The undecided will eventually decide, and they will base that decision on what they observe rather than what they are told. The third, and perhaps the most costly, is ignoring the undecided and the quietly cautious. These groups rarely demand attention, which means they rarely receive it. Yet their eventual positioning often determines whether the program achieves broad adoption or remains the project of a committed few.

Maintaining a dynamic map requires establishing habits rather than processes. The most useful practice is to build a brief reassessment into the rhythm of the program's regular cadence, asking at each major milestone or governance checkpoint: whose position has shifted since the last assessment, what prompted the shift, and what does that shift imply for the next phase of engagement? Specific triggers should prompt an unscheduled review: unexpected resistance in a governance forum, a change in leadership within a key stakeholder group, a missed milestone that increases pressure on the program, or informal signals that a coalition's composition or posture has changed. The goal is not to produce a perfect real-time picture, which is unattainable, but to prevent the map from drifting so far from reality that it stops being useful for planning conversations and anticipating risks.

Working Through Informal Networks

The formal channels of a transformation program, its governance bodies, steering committees, status reports, and working groups, are necessary but insufficient for building and maintaining alignment. They provide structure, accountability, and a record of decisions. What they do not provide is access to the informal networks through which much of the organization's actual sense-making occurs.

Every organization contains individuals who serve as nodes in these informal networks: people whose opinions are sought before others commit, who mediate disagreements before they reach formal channels, or who anchor the shared interpretation of events within their part of the organization. These individuals may or may not hold senior titles. What they hold is trust, built through years of consistent judgment, reliable relationships, and demonstrated competence. When these individuals shift their position on a transformation, their movement ripples outward through the network in ways that amplify far beyond their formal authority.

Working with informal networks does not mean circumventing formal governance. It means recognizing that formal structures operate within a social context and that the effectiveness of formal decisions depends on whether they are supported, interpreted, and carried forward through the informal relationships that connect people across the organization. A decision ratified in a steering committee will be implemented by teams whose understanding of that decision is shaped as much by conversations in hallways, on messaging platforms, and during working lunches as by the official minutes.

For transformation leaders, this means investing in relationships with the people who occupy influential positions within informal networks, not to co-opt them but to ensure that they are well-informed, that their concerns are understood, and that they have access to the reasoning behind key decisions. It also means paying attention to the signals that travel through these networks. When informal channels begin carrying a narrative that diverges from the program's official messaging, the informal narrative is usually more influential. Engaging with it directly, rather than attempting to override it with more formal communication, is almost always the more effective response.

The reason teams sometimes act cautiously even when they support the transformation is often traceable to these informal dynamics. An individual may personally believe in the change but observe that respected colleagues are hesitant, that the informal consensus within their network is skeptical, or that the social cost of early adoption is higher than the social cost of waiting. In these situations, working through the informal network to provide credible reassurance, to demonstrate that concerns are being taken seriously, or to create visible evidence that early engagement is safe and valued, can unlock movement that no amount of formal communication would produce.

The stakeholder ecosystem is not a backdrop to transformation. It is the medium through which transformation occurs. Every agreement, every shift in alignment, every instance of resistance or cooperation takes place within this network of relationships, interests, and influence. Understanding the ecosystem, reading its signals, maintaining an accurate and current map of its dynamics, and engaging with it through both formal and informal channels is a foundational requirement for any leader who intends to build alignment that endures. That engagement becomes possible only when leaders can look past what stakeholders say they want and identify what they actually need.

PART II
CORE SKILLS

Chapter 4

Interests vs. Positions: The Core Skill

The meeting was the fourth in a series convened to resolve the governance structure for a newly merged risk and compliance function. The two departments had operated independently for over a decade, each with its own leadership, its own processes, and its own reporting relationships. The merger had been approved at the executive level as part of a broader organizational simplification initiative, and the business case was sound: reduced duplication, clearer accountability, stronger regulatory posture. What remained unresolved was how the combined function would be governed, and it was this question that had consumed the four meetings without producing agreement.

The head of the legacy risk team, a woman named Priya who had built the function over eight years, argued that the combined unit should retain dual reporting lines to preserve the independence of risk assessment from compliance operations. The head of compliance, David, maintained that a single reporting line to the Chief Operating Officer was essential for operational clarity and that dual reporting would introduce confusion and delay. Both positions were articulated with precision and defended with genuine conviction. Both were also, by the fourth meeting, entirely familiar to everyone in the room. The conversation had taken on a circular quality. Each session revisited the same arguments, refined them slightly, and ended with an agreement to continue the discussion at the next meeting.

It was the program director, who had been observing the pattern across the four sessions, who changed the trajectory of the conversation. She did not challenge either position. Instead, she asked Priya a question that had not been asked before: "If we could design a governance structure that guaranteed your team's analytical independence, regardless of the reporting line, what would that need to look like?" The room went quiet for a moment. Priya's response, when it came, was noticeably different in character from the arguments she had been making. She spoke about the credibility of the risk function, about how it had earned its reputation through years of producing assessments that were trusted precisely because they were seen as independent from operational pressures. She spoke about the concern that merging into a single reporting line would, over time, subordinate risk judgment to compliance efficiency. She was no longer arguing about reporting lines. She was describing what the reporting lines meant to her and to her team.

David listened, and when he responded, his tone shifted as well. He acknowledged that his own concern was not really about operational clarity in the abstract. It was about ensuring that the combined function could move quickly on regulatory matters without being slowed by a governance structure that required constant negotiation between two leadership tracks. What he wanted was responsiveness. What Priya wanted was credibility. These were not incompatible needs, but they had been invisible for four meetings because the conversation had never moved past the positions that concealed them.

The distinction between positions and interests is the most consequential skill in the practice of internal negotiation. Positions describe what someone says they want. Interests explain why they want it. The ability to move from one to the other determines whether a transformation advances through genuine alignment or becomes trapped in the kind of circular debate that consumed those four governance meetings.

Why Positions Fail

Positions represent the declarative layer of a stakeholder's demand. They are shaped by what individuals feel comfortable stating publicly, what their roles require them to defend, and how they believe others expect them to behave. A position typically appears as a firm stance: a department insists on retaining a particular process, a leader rejects a proposed timeline, a team requests additional resources as a precondition for participation. These statements carry real weight. They reflect genuine concerns, and they deserve to be taken seriously. But they also tend to be brittle in ways that become apparent only when they are tested.

A position holds as long as the individual feels that the underlying concern it protects has not been touched. When conditions change, when a new option emerges, or when the conversation shifts to address what the position was actually guarding, the position itself often becomes negotiable. This is why debates that focus exclusively on stated positions tend to become circular. Each party repeats what it wants without examining why it wants it, and the conversation revolves around what cannot be changed rather than around what must be protected. The governance dispute in the opening example followed this pattern precisely. The positions were clear. The interests were hidden. And the conversation could not advance until someone created the conditions for those interests to surface.

The most visible failures of position-based negotiation occur during cross-functional alignment, where different groups bring genuinely different priorities and where each group's position is shaped by a distinct set of pressures. A department insisting on keeping a process local may appear intransigent to the program team. A function demanding more headcount before it can participate may appear to be stalling. A regional leader rejecting the recommended timeline may appear to be obstructing progress. In each case, the position is real, but the motivation behind it is more complex and more addressable than the position itself suggests. When the negotiation stays at the level of positions, the discussion becomes a contest of wills. When it moves to the level of interests, the discussion becomes a search for solutions.

Table 6

Positions and Interests in Practical Negotiation

Concept	Description	Typical Characteristics	Implications for Transformation Negotiation
Position	The explicit statement of what a stakeholder claims to want. It represents the surface-level demand expressed in meetings or documents.	Declarative, often rigid in tone; shaped by role expectations; influenced by what feels acceptable to state publicly; may oversimplify underlying concerns.	Negotiation that focuses solely on positions becomes circular and brittle; agreements formed at the level of positions lack durability; repeated debates occur because the real drivers of resistance remain unaddressed.
Interest	The underlying motivation that explains why the stakeholder holds a particular position. It reflects functional needs, personal concerns, identity considerations, or political dynamics.	Stable over time; emotionally meaningful; flexible in how it can be satisfied; often unspoken or only partially articulated; revealed through behavior, tone, and context.	Negotiation that identifies and addresses interests produces more sustainable alignment; alternative solutions become visible; stakeholders show greater willingness to adjust positions; agreements become more resilient in changing conditions.

Why Interests Endure

Interests endure because they describe the actual motivations that drive behavior. Where positions are declarations, interests are the needs, fears, constraints, and aspirations that persist even when the specific terms of a discussion change. A department head who insists on retaining a legacy process may adjust her position if the interest that motivated it, say, protecting her team's capacity to serve local clients during the transition, is addressed through a different mechanism. The position was the vehicle. The interest is the destination.

Four categories of interest recur most frequently in transformation contexts. Recognizing them helps leaders interpret what they are actually hearing.

Functional interests arise from the operational realities of a team's work. They include concerns about process stability, resource predictability, throughput capacity, and the ability to meet existing performance commitments while absorbing new demands. A finance team's interest in maintaining quarterly close processes without disruption is functional. An operations team's interest in preserving supplier relationships during a systems transition is functional. These interests are rational and generally predictable, but they collide with each other during transformation because each function evaluates change through the lens of its own operational requirements.

Political interests emerge from the distribution of influence within the organization. Certain groups may wish to maintain decision-making authority over domains they have historically controlled. Others may seek increased visibility or stronger participation in strategic discussions. A leader who has spent years building a center of excellence may view a restructuring as a threat to the influence that center carries. Another may see the same restructuring as an opportunity to expand her team's role. These interests are not inherently negative. They reflect the need to safeguard the conditions under which teams can perform effectively and leaders can exercise the judgment they were hired to provide. But they complicate transformation when they remain unacknowledged, because they shape behavior in ways that purely operational analysis cannot explain.

Personal interests grow from individual circumstances. Concerns about workload, career trajectory, perceived risk, or the capacity to acquire new skills all fall into this category. Personal interests shape how individuals interpret timelines, responsibilities, and expectations. Even highly committed employees may hesitate when they fear being overwhelmed by new demands or exposed by unfamiliar requirements. A senior analyst who has built her career on expertise in a legacy system may support the transformation intellectually while fearing that the transition will render her most valuable skills obsolete. These personal stakes are rarely discussed openly, but they exert powerful influence on the pace and quality of engagement.

Identity-based interests cut deeper than any other category. They involve the meaning that individuals attach to their professional role, their sense of competence, and the reputation they have built within the organization. Priya's concern about the risk function's credibility was an identity-based interest. It was not about reporting lines or operational efficiency. It was about what her team stood for and how it was perceived. A leader who built his reputation on a particular approach to client service may struggle to support a redesign that renders that approach obsolete, not because the redesign is wrong but because it threatens the narrative he has constructed about his own contribution. A team known for its reliability may resist a process change that introduces uncertainty into their performance, not because they oppose improvement but because reliability is central to how they understand themselves.

Any given position may draw from several of these categories simultaneously. A seemingly procedural concern about governance may conceal identity-based fears about diminished status. A request for additional resources may stem from functional pressure compounded by personal worry about being asked to deliver beyond capacity. Recognizing that interests are layered, that they often interact and reinforce each other, strengthens the foundation for productive negotiation because it prevents leaders from mistaking the resolution of one interest for the resolution of the whole.

How Unspoken Fears Shape Stated Demands

Unspoken fears exert powerful influence over how people articulate their positions. These fears rarely surface directly in organizational conversation. Individuals avoid expressing them because they worry about appearing resistant, insecure, or insufficiently committed to the program. In many organizational cultures, admitting to fear, whether about workload, competence, relevance, or control, carries a social cost that most people are unwilling to pay. So the fears find other channels. They emerge not as statements but as patterns.

A fear of losing control over key decisions often manifests as a demand for exceptions. The individual does not say "I am afraid of becoming irrelevant in this new structure." Instead, they argue that their area requires a tailored approach due to its unique complexity. A fear of being judged unprepared for new responsibilities translates into constant requests for clarity, for additional briefings, for written confirmation of expectations that others seem willing to accept verbally. A fear of workload overload produces cautious, incremental movement even from individuals who express full support for the initiative. They agree to everything in principle and advance nothing in practice, not out of opposition but out of a quiet calculation that moving slowly is safer than moving at a pace that risks failure.

These patterns become visible to leaders who know what to look for. A repeated reference to past experiences, particularly past failures, often signals a fear that the current transformation will reproduce an earlier painful outcome. A tone shift during discussion of specific implementation details, where a stakeholder becomes noticeably more guarded or more precise in their language, may indicate that the conversation has moved close to a concern they are not prepared to articulate directly. A contrast between stated enthusiasm and observable behavior, where someone voices strong support but consistently defers action, is one of the most reliable indicators that an unspoken fear is shaping their engagement.

Negotiation that accounts for these unspoken elements does not require leaders to play the role of therapist. It requires creating conditions where the real concerns can surface without penalty. Sometimes this means asking a question that gives the stakeholder permission to express a concern indirectly: "What would need to be true for this to feel manageable for your team?" Sometimes it means demonstrating through action that concerns are taken seriously: adjusting a timeline, providing additional support, or restructuring responsibilities in a way that addresses the fear without requiring anyone to name it explicitly. The goal is not to force hidden fears into the open but to create enough safety that the interests driving behavior become accessible to the negotiation.

Three Scenarios in Practice

The distinction between positions and interests becomes most visible in specific situations, where the abstract framework meets the texture of real organizational life.

In a technology adoption scenario during a financial services transformation, the head of client operations, a director named Elena, insisted that a new portfolio management platform be introduced in phases rather than through a single enterprise-wide deployment. Her position was clear and consistently stated: a phased approach was the only responsible path. The program team initially interpreted this as conservatism and pushed back with data showing that a phased rollout would cost more and extend the timeline by nearly a year. Elena did not budge. It was only when her deputy, during a working session focused on training logistics, mentioned that several senior analysts on the team had never worked with a cloud-based platform and were concerned about their ability to maintain client service standards during the transition, that the underlying interest became visible. Elena was not opposed to the platform. She was protecting her team from a transition that threatened to expose skill gaps in front of clients. Once this interest was understood, the conversation shifted. The program team designed a targeted capability-building program for the analysts most affected, provided a temporary support structure during the initial months, and adjusted the rollout sequence to allow Elena's team to build confidence before the highest-visibility client accounts were migrated. Elena accepted a compressed timeline that she had previously rejected, because the interest that her original position was protecting had been addressed through a different mechanism.

In a regional exception scenario, the country manager for a Latin American subsidiary of a global consumer products company requested that his market be exempted from a standardized procurement model being rolled out across all regions. His stated position was that local supplier relationships were too complex and too relationship-dependent to be managed through a centralized system. The global program team viewed this as a familiar pattern of regional resistance to standardization and initially responded with a presentation demonstrating the efficiency gains achieved in other markets. The country manager listened politely and restated his request. The breakthrough came when a member of the program team spent two days in the regional office and observed how procurement actually operated on the ground. The local team's supplier relationships were not merely transactional. They were embedded in a network of personal connections, reciprocal commitments, and cultural norms that had taken years to build and that the centralized model had no mechanism to preserve. The country manager's interest was not in avoiding accountability or resisting change. It was in protecting a set of relationships that he believed were essential to his market's performance and that he feared would be damaged by a system designed without understanding of how they functioned. The resolution involved adapting the centralized model to preserve the relationship management layer for key local suppliers while integrating the back-end processes into the global standard. The country manager became one of the program's most effective regional advocates, precisely because his core interest had been taken seriously rather than overridden.

The functional merger scenario, which opened this chapter, illustrates how identity-based interests operate. Priya and David were not arguing about governance for its own sake. Priya was protecting the credibility and independence that defined her team's identity. David was protecting the operational responsiveness that he believed would determine the combined function's success. Once these interests were named, the solution was not difficult to design: an independent review mechanism for risk assessments that reported to the board's risk committee, combined with a streamlined operational workflow under a single management line for compliance execution. Both interests were satisfied. Neither position, as originally stated, was adopted. The structure that emerged was better than either leader had proposed because it was designed to address what they actually needed rather than what they had initially demanded.

Across these three examples, the lesson is consistent. Positions describe the surface. Interests explain the structure beneath it. The ability to move from one to the other is what separates negotiation that produces durable alignment from negotiation that produces agreements destined to unravel under the first real pressure. What makes that skill systematic is a set of structured tools for mapping interests, testing assumptions, and converting what is observed and inferred into a practical foundation for more productive conversations.

Chapter 5

Mapping Interests: Tools for Revealing What Stakeholders Really Need

The program director for the portfolio management platform migration sat down at her desk on a Tuesday evening with a notebook, a cup of coffee that was already cold, and a problem she could not yet fully articulate. In two days she would meet with Elena, the head of client operations whose insistence on a phased rollout had become the program's most significant unresolved negotiation. The previous chapter described how Elena's deputy had inadvertently revealed the interest beneath the position: the team's concern about capability gaps being exposed during the transition. That revelation had shifted the conversation, but it had also raised new questions. If the capability concern was real, how deep did it run? Was it the only driver, or were there additional interests that had not yet surfaced? Were there members of Elena's team whose concerns differed from hers? And were there conditions under which Elena's position might shift further than anyone currently expected?

The program director had information, but it was scattered. Some of it came from formal meetings. Some came from side comments overheard during working sessions. Some came from the tone Elena used when discussing certain aspects of the timeline, a tone that shifted perceptibly when the conversation moved from general strategy to specific implementation milestones. Individually, none of these observations amounted to a clear picture. Together, they suggested something more complex than a single concern about skills. The challenge was to organize what she knew, identify what she suspected, and clarify what she still needed to learn, all before walking into a meeting where the quality of her preparation would determine whether the conversation produced movement or another round of polite stalemate.

This chapter introduces the tools that make that kind of preparation systematic. Interests often remain partially hidden, expressed through caution, hesitation, or signals that are easy to miss in the flow of organizational life. The challenge for any transformation leader is to convert those scattered signals into structured understanding. Mapping techniques do this by turning informal observations into coherent frameworks that improve the quality of preparation, shape more productive conversations, and strengthen the foundation on which durable alignment is built.

The Interest Map Framework

The Interest Map provides a structured method for interpreting the forces that shape a stakeholder's position. It is not a diagnostic form to be completed once and filed. It is a working tool that develops over time as new information becomes available, as conversations reveal new dimensions, and as the stakeholder's own circumstances evolve.

The map begins with the stated position at its center. This is the explicit demand, request, or objection that the stakeholder has expressed, placed at the center not because it is the most important element but because it serves as the anchor for everything else. The inquiry radiates outward from this anchor, asking: what does this position protect, what does it avoid, and what does it seek to gain?

Branches extend from the center to capture the interests that may explain the position. Some branches represent what the stakeholder is trying to protect: a workflow, the stability of a team, a reputation for reliability, or a set of relationships that the transformation threatens to disrupt. Other branches represent what the stakeholder hopes to avoid: increased exposure to risk, disruption to operations they are accountable for, loss of decision-making authority, or the experience of being judged on unfamiliar terms. Still other branches capture anticipated benefits or aspirations: opportunities for greater influence, improved efficiency, alignment with long-term professional goals, or recognition that a new structure might provide. Each interest appears as a separate node because each carries its own sources of motivation and may require a different approach during negotiation.

One of the framework's most important features is its treatment of uncertainty. Not every interest is equally visible or equally well understood. The map addresses this by assigning each interest a confidence level. Confirmed interests are those that the stakeholder has expressed directly or demonstrated consistently through behavior and decisions. Probable interests are inferred from context, from patterns observed in earlier interactions, or from the stakeholder's history, but have not been explicitly stated. Speculative interests are hypotheses that remain untested, requiring further conversation or observation before they can be relied upon. This confidence layer prevents the map from presenting guesses with the same weight as established facts, and it guides the leader toward the questions that will improve the map's accuracy over time.

The side-by-side structure of the map reveals relationships between interests that might not be obvious when each concern is held separately in memory. A worry about workload may connect to a deeper concern about professional credibility. A desire for exceptions in a standardized process may link to an anxiety about losing the autonomy that defines how a team sees itself. These connections become visible when interests are arranged in proximity rather than processed sequentially in conversation. In some cases, the map also reveals patterns across stakeholders. Different individuals or groups may share similar underlying concerns even when they express them in entirely different terms, and recognizing these overlaps opens possibilities for coordinated engagement and solutions that address multiple interests simultaneously.

Table 7.

Core Elements of the Interest Map Framework

Concept	Description	Purpose Within the Framework	Practical Implications for Negotiation
Central Position	The explicit request, refusal, or declarative stance stated by the stakeholder.	Serves as the anchor for analysis and frames the inquiry into what lies beneath the visible statement.	Helps prevent premature interpretation; keeps attention focused on the underlying meaning behind the stated demand.
Interest Branches	Nodes representing what the stakeholder seeks to protect, avoid, or gain. Includes operational concerns, risks, and desired benefits.	Reveals the motivations and pressures shaping the position; separates distinct drivers for clarity.	Offers multiple pathways for negotiation by showing how different adjustments might address specific concerns.
Confirmed Interests	Interests expressed directly or demonstrated consistently through words and actions.	Provide the most reliable foundation for building agreements.	Guide the design of solutions that address clear and acknowledged needs.
Probable Interests	Interests inferred from context, patterns, or the stakeholder's history, yet not explicitly stated.	Highlight areas requiring further exploration or validation.	Encourage targeted questions that refine understanding and prevent misinterpretation.
Speculative Interests	Possible motivations that remain uncertain and require careful testing.	Expand the range of hypotheses when limited information is available.	Prevent assumptions from becoming rigid; support flexible inquiry and deeper listening.
Cross-Interest Connections	Relationships among interests, such as risk concerns linking to identity needs or autonomy concerns linking to workload protection.	Reveal patterns that influence how the stakeholder interprets the transformation.	Enable integrated solutions that address multiple interests simultaneously.
Overlap Across Stakeholders	Similar interests detected in multiple groups, even when expressed differently.	Identifies shared motivations that can support coordinated negotiation.	Creates opportunities for collective agreements and broader alignment-building strategies.

Building the Map: A Worked Example

The program director opened her notebook and wrote Elena's stated position at the center of a blank page: "Phased rollout only. Enterprise-wide deployment is not acceptable." Around it, she began noting what she already knew.

In the initial version of the map, built from formal meeting discussions and the program team's existing understanding, three interests appeared. The first was operational continuity: Elena's team managed high-value client portfolios, and any disruption to service delivery during the transition would carry immediate and measurable consequences. This was a confirmed interest, stated explicitly in multiple forums. The second was resource adequacy: Elena had raised questions about whether her team would receive sufficient training and temporary support during the migration. This was also confirmed, though less forcefully stated. The third was the capability concern that her deputy had surfaced, the fear that the new platform would expose skill gaps among senior analysts who had worked exclusively with the legacy system. The program director marked this as probable. Elena had not confirmed it directly, but her deputy's comment, combined with Elena's visible discomfort when the conversation turned to individual readiness assessments, made the inference credible.

This initial map was useful but incomplete. It explained the position but did not yet reveal whether there were conditions under which it might shift.

The developed version of the map emerged after a one-on-one conversation the program director held with Elena two days later. The conversation was deliberately exploratory rather than persuasive. The program director did not argue for a different rollout approach. Instead, she asked what Elena's primary concerns would be even if a phased rollout were approved, reasoning that the answer would reveal interests that the phased position was not fully addressing. Elena's response was revealing. She spoke at length about accountability. If the migration went poorly in her area, she would bear the reputational consequences regardless of the rollout method. She mentioned, almost in passing, that a previous system migration five years earlier had resulted in client complaints that took months to resolve and that her predecessor had been reassigned in the aftermath. This was new information. The program director added two nodes to the map: a probable interest in reputational protection, connected to the confirmed interest in operational continuity, and a speculative interest in career safety, inferred from the reference to the predecessor's reassignment. She also upgraded the capability concern from probable to confirmed, because Elena's responses throughout the conversation consistently returned to her team's readiness as the factor she felt least confident about.

The revised version came together over the following week, after the program director paid attention to several informal signals. During a break in a cross-functional workshop, Elena's project coordinator mentioned to a colleague that Elena had been asking her team leads to document their current workflows in unusual detail, a behavior consistent with someone preparing to defend established practices. At a social event, Elena made a brief comment to the program director about wanting to "make sure my people don't get lost in the shuffle," a phrase that suggested a concern about the team's visibility and identity within the larger organizational change. The program director added a speculative node for team identity, noting its possible connection to the reputational protection interest. She also noted that the workflow documentation behavior might indicate a new interest she had not anticipated: Elena might be building a case for retaining certain legacy processes within the new system, an interest in preserving specific operational elements rather than opposing the platform itself.

The map now contained eight interest nodes across three confidence levels, with several connections between them. It was not a finished picture. But it was detailed enough to guide the next conversation with a degree of precision that the program director's initial understanding could not have supported.

The Art of the Probing Question

The quality of an Interest Map depends on the quality of the conversations that inform it. Probing questions are the primary instrument for improving that quality, but they must be handled with care. A question that feels like a challenge to the stakeholder's position will produce defensiveness. A question that feels like genuine curiosity about the stakeholder's situation will produce information.

The most effective approach follows a natural progression, beginning with broad exploration and narrowing toward specific conditions. The opening questions should be genuinely open and oriented toward understanding rather than testing. A question like "What would need to be true for this transition to feel workable for your team?" invites the stakeholder to describe the conditions they need without forcing them to defend or abandon their current position. It communicates interest in their reality rather than impatience with their stance. Early in a conversation, questions of this kind establish the tone and signal that the discussion is oriented toward problem-solving rather than persuasion.

As the conversation develops and the stakeholder becomes more specific about their concerns, the questions can become more targeted. "If we were able to address the training gap before the migration begins, how would that change your view of the timeline?" probes a specific constraint and tests whether it is a genuine barrier or a proxy for something deeper. If the stakeholder responds with openness, the constraint was likely real. If they respond by shifting to a different concern, the original constraint may have been a surface expression of a more fundamental interest. Either response is valuable.

The final stage of probing tests flexibility directly, though always within the frame of collaboration rather than pressure. "If we could guarantee that your team's client-facing performance metrics would be held harmless during the first six months, would that change what feels possible?" This kind of question proposes a specific condition and asks the stakeholder to evaluate it. The answer reveals not only whether the particular condition matters but how the stakeholder weighs different interests against each other. If a guarantee of performance protection does not shift the position, the driving interest is probably not operational at all. It may be reputational, political, or identity-based, and the map should be updated accordingly.

Reading the Signals Between the Words

Stakeholders reveal more through their behavior than through their explicit statements, and the signals that matter most are often the ones that occur outside the structure of formal discussions. A hesitation before answering a direct question about readiness may indicate uncertainty about workload that the stakeholder has not yet fully processed. A repeated return to past experiences, particularly past failures, carries information about what the stakeholder fears will happen again. A sudden and specific enthusiasm for a minor adjustment, when the stakeholder has been cautious about everything else, hints at a desire for autonomy or recognition that the larger conversation has not addressed.

Side comments deserve particular attention. The remarks that people make after a meeting has formally ended, during a walk to the elevator, or in the margins of an unrelated conversation often carry more emotional honesty than anything said during the meeting itself. These are the moments when the filter relaxes slightly, when the stakeholder speaks from their actual experience rather than from the position they have constructed for public consumption. Elena's comment about not wanting her people to "get lost in the shuffle" was exactly this kind of signal. It was brief, casual, and easily overlooked. But it pointed toward an interest, team identity and visibility, that had not appeared in any formal discussion and that turned out to be an important piece of the picture.

Recording these signals alongside stated interests enriches the map and makes it a more accurate representation of the full motivational landscape. A map that contains only what stakeholders have said in meetings is a map of positions. A map that also captures behavioral observations, tonal shifts, and informal remarks is a map that begins to approach the level of interests.

Testing Scenarios Against the Map

Once the Interest Map has reached a reasonable level of development, scenario testing allows the leader to explore how different responses might affect the stakeholder's position. The method is straightforward: imagine a specific change in conditions, trace its implications through the map, and assess whether the position would likely soften, hold firm, or shift in a new direction.

If removing workload uncertainty leads to greater openness, then targeted support is the most effective lever, and the driving interest is operational. If offering governance adjustments produces more movement than offering resources, the driving interest is political or related to autonomy. If nothing the leader can imagine seems to shift the position, identity-based concerns or deep structural tensions are likely at play, and the negotiation will require a different kind of engagement, one that addresses meaning and recognition rather than logistics and resources.

Scenario testing also helps identify leverage points that might not be obvious from the map alone. The program director's discovery that Elena might be interested in preserving specific legacy workflows, rather than opposing the platform wholesale, opened a negotiation pathway that neither party had previously considered. By testing the scenario of partial process retention against Elena's mapped interests, the program director could assess whether such an offer would address enough of the interest landscape to shift the overall position. In Elena's case, it did, because it addressed operational continuity, team identity, and capability concerns simultaneously.

The discipline of scenario testing also reveals which interests carry the most weight. When a hypothetical change addresses one interest but leaves the position unchanged, the untouched interests are the ones that matter most. This is useful diagnostic information that prevents leaders from investing negotiation effort in areas that will not produce results.

Keeping the Map Current

An Interest Map is not a deliverable to be completed and archived. It evolves as the transformation progresses and as the stakeholder's circumstances change. A static map becomes an artifact of outdated assumptions, and decisions guided by it will misread the landscape in ways that erode trust and waste the opportunity to course-correct before positions harden.

Revision involves returning to each interest on the map and asking whether it remains accurate in light of recent behavior, conversations, and developments. A speculative interest may become confirmed when the stakeholder's actions consistently reflect it. A confirmed interest may recede in importance as the conditions that produced it change. New interests may appear as the transformation enters a new phase and introduces demands that were not relevant during earlier stages. The capability concern that dominated Elena's map in the early months might diminish once training is underway, only to be replaced by a new concern about how performance will be measured during the transition, an interest that did not exist when the map was first drawn.

The most practical approach is to build map revision into the program's existing rhythm. Before any significant conversation with a key stakeholder, review the map and update it with anything observed since the last revision. After the conversation, record new information immediately, while the details are fresh. At major program milestones, conduct a broader review across all active maps to identify shifts in the stakeholder landscape that individual conversations might not have revealed. The goal is not cartographic perfection. It is the habit of structured attention to how the people around the transformation are experiencing it, what they need, and how those needs are changing over time.

When used consistently, Interest Maps transform the preparation process. They shift the focus from rehearsing arguments to understanding the person across the table. They provide a disciplined method for converting scattered observations into a coherent picture. And they give the transformation leader something that intuition alone cannot reliably provide: a structured, testable, updatable account of what it will take for each stakeholder to participate fully and confidently in the work ahead. What determines what leaders can do with that understanding is the negotiation structure itself: the alternatives available when talks fail, the space within which agreement is possible, and the sources of influence that shape which outcomes hold.

Chapter 6
Leverage, BATNA, and ZOPA Inside the Organization

The change leader responsible for a global operating model redesign had reached the point in the program where the theoretical alignment secured months earlier was about to be tested by a concrete decision. The new model called for standardized regional operations across five markets, governed by a single process framework with shared service centers handling transactional work. The executive sponsor, a member of the C-suite with board visibility on the initiative, wanted the model deployed simultaneously across all five regions within twelve months. Three of the five regional heads had, in various ways, signaled that this timeline was not workable. Their objections differed in specifics but converged on a common theme: the pace was unrealistic given local complexities, and they wanted either a delayed start or a phased approach that would begin with a pilot in one or two regions before expanding.

The change leader, a program director named Tomás who reported to the sponsor and worked daily with the regional teams, understood both sides of the argument. The sponsor's urgency was genuine. The board had approved the investment on the basis of a twelve-month timeline, and any visible delay would raise questions about execution capability. The regional heads' concerns were also genuine. Two of the markets were managing simultaneous regulatory changes that would compete for the same leadership attention the operating model required. The third had recently experienced turnover in its operations leadership and lacked the bench strength to absorb a major transition without additional support.

Tomás needed to prepare for a series of conversations that would determine the program's trajectory. But before he could negotiate effectively, he needed to answer three questions that most transformation leaders encounter but few approach with the discipline they require. First, what would actually happen if no agreement was reached? Not the hypothetical worst case, but the realistic alternative that each party would pursue if the current negotiation failed to produce a workable outcome. Second, was there a range of outcomes that all parties could accept, and if so, how wide or narrow was that range? Third, what sources of influence did each party actually hold, and how might those shift as the program progressed? These three questions correspond to three concepts from negotiation theory that, when adapted for internal organizational use, provide a degree of strategic clarity that intuition alone cannot match.

BATNA Inside the Organization

In classical negotiation theory, BATNA refers to a party's best alternative to a negotiated agreement. It is what you will do if the current negotiation fails to produce an acceptable result. In external negotiations, this concept is relatively straightforward. A buyer whose negotiation with one supplier stalls can turn to another supplier. A job candidate who cannot reach acceptable terms with one employer can accept an offer from a different one. The BATNA provides a reference point: any agreement that is worse than the alternative should be rejected, and any agreement that is better than the alternative has value.

Inside organizations, the concept requires reinterpretation. No one walks away from an internal negotiation in the way that a buyer walks away from a supplier. The parties will continue to work together regardless of the outcome. But alternatives still exist, and they shape behavior just as powerfully as they do in external settings. The difference is that internal BATNAs tend to be less explicit, more varied in form, and more consequential for long-term relationships.

Consider the parties in Tomás's situation. The executive sponsor's BATNA, if the regional heads refused to commit to the twelve-month timeline, was escalation. She could take the matter to the CEO, invoke the board mandate, and direct the regions to comply. This alternative was available to her, and everyone involved knew it. But it carried significant costs: it would consume political capital, signal to the organization that alignment on the program was weaker than advertised, and create compliance-driven adoption rather than committed engagement. It was a real alternative, but not an attractive one.

The regional heads' BATNAs were subtler and, in some ways, more powerful. Their most likely alternative to agreement was not open defiance but the pattern described in Chapter 2 as quiet refusal: participating formally while withholding the discretionary effort that determines whether a new operating model actually takes root. They could attend governance meetings, submit status reports, and assign staff to project activities while quietly ensuring that the real adoption work proceeded at a pace they controlled. This form of passive non-compliance is an internal BATNA that is extraordinarily common and extraordinarily difficult to counter through formal authority alone, because it produces no visible act of resistance that can be addressed directly.

Tomás's own BATNA was to restructure the program. If full agreement on the twelve-month timeline proved impossible, he could propose a modified approach: launch in two regions where readiness was strongest, establish a review gate at six months, and use the results to build the case for expansion. This alternative was less ambitious than the sponsor's preferred outcome but more realistic than the regional heads' preferred delay, and it had the advantage of producing early evidence that could shift the dynamics of later negotiations.

Understanding these BATNAs changed how Tomás prepared for the conversations ahead. Knowing that the sponsor's escalation option was available but costly told him that she had strong leverage but limited willingness to use it without first exhausting collaborative options. Knowing that the regional heads' most likely alternative was passive non-compliance told him that forcing agreement through authority would not actually solve the problem, because compliance and commitment are fundamentally different outcomes. And knowing his own restructuring option gave him psychological steadiness. He was not dependent on any single outcome. He had a viable path regardless of how the conversations unfolded, and that knowledge allowed him to negotiate from a position of clarity rather than anxiety.

The psychological dimension of BATNA analysis is the one most frequently overlooked. Leaders who enter negotiations without understanding their alternatives tend to negotiate reactively, making concessions under pressure because they fear the consequences of deadlock. Leaders who have thought carefully about what happens if agreement fails negotiate with a different quality of attention. They can listen more openly, probe more patiently, and hold firmer on matters that genuinely require it, because they are not operating from a position of dependence on any particular outcome.

Table 8.

BATNA Analysis Framework

Stakeholder	Stated Position	Likely BATNA if No Agreement	Estimated Tolerance Range	Implications for Negotiation Strategy
Executive Sponsor	Full rollout across all five regions within twelve months.	Escalation to CEO; invoke board mandate to direct compliance. Effective but costly to political capital and long-term engagement quality.	May accept a fourteen-to-sixteen-month timeline if early momentum is visible and board communication is managed.	Needs evidence that any modified timeline will not be perceived as program weakness. Frame alternatives as acceleration strategies rather than delays.
Regional Head (Market A)	Delayed start of at least six months due to concurrent regulatory changes.	Passive non-compliance; formal participation with minimal substantive adoption.	Could accept an earlier start if regulatory workload is offset by additional temporary resources.	Address the resource constraint directly. A delayed start is the position; manageable workload is the interest.
Regional Head (Market B)	Pilot approach; wants to observe results before committing to full deployment.	Wait-and-see posture; slow engagement while citing the need for evidence of viability.	Likely to accept earlier participation if given visible input into the design and a formal review mechanism.	Leverage the desire for influence. Offer design participation in exchange for earlier commitment.

ZOPA: Finding the Space Where Agreement Exists

If BATNA defines what happens when agreement fails, ZOPA defines the space within which agreement is possible. The zone of possible agreement is the overlap between what each party can accept. Any outcome that falls within this zone is, by definition, better for all parties than their respective alternatives. The negotiation challenge is to identify whether this zone exists, how wide it is, and where within it the final agreement should land.

In transformation contexts, the ZOPA is often wider than the parties assume. This is because positional negotiation, where each side states a preferred outcome and defends it, tends to obscure the range of acceptable outcomes that lies between the stated positions. The sponsor who insists on twelve months and the regional head who requests eighteen months may both be able to accept a fourteen-month timeline with specific conditions attached, but neither will discover this if the conversation remains anchored to the stated numbers.

The ZOPA becomes visible when the negotiation moves from positions to interests, which is why the skill developed in Chapter 4 is a prerequisite for the analysis presented here. When Tomás understood that the sponsor's core interest was demonstrating momentum to the board, not adherence to the specific twelve-month number, and that the regional heads' core interests centered on workload manageability, leadership capacity, and design input rather than on delay for its own sake, the zone of possible agreement expanded considerably. A timeline that demonstrated early momentum while accommodating legitimate capacity constraints could satisfy both sets of interests, even though it matched neither party's stated position.

Sometimes the ZOPA is genuinely narrow. When the interests at stake involve zero-sum dynamics, such as the allocation of a fixed budget between competing priorities, or when identity-based interests make any concession feel like a loss of standing, the overlap between acceptable outcomes may be thin. In these situations, creative expansion of the ZOPA becomes the leader's primary task. Linking the current negotiation to a separate issue, adjusting the sequencing of commitments so that early concessions are balanced by later gains, or introducing new terms that address an interest not previously on the table can all widen the zone enough to make agreement possible.

Sometimes no ZOPA exists at all. This is less common than most negotiators fear, but it does occur. When interests are genuinely incompatible, when one party's minimum acceptable outcome exceeds what the other party can offer even under the most creative terms, the leader faces a fundamentally different kind of decision. The options in this situation are explored later in this chapter.

What Gives Each Party Influence

Leverage is the third concept that completes the analytical framework, and it is the one most frequently misunderstood in internal organizational contexts. Leverage is commonly associated with power, but the two are not identical. Power is the capacity to act. Leverage is the capacity to influence the outcome of a specific negotiation. A senior executive has organizational power by virtue of her position. Whether she has leverage in a particular negotiation depends on what she controls that the other party needs and what alternatives exist if she chooses not to exercise that control.

Inside organizations, leverage takes several forms. Control over resources, whether financial, human, or technological, provides leverage when the other party depends on those resources to achieve their objectives. Technical expertise provides leverage when the transformation requires specialized knowledge that only certain individuals or teams possess. Relationships with senior leadership provide leverage because they confer access to decision-making authority and the ability to shape how information reaches the top of the organization. Gatekeeping of critical information, whether market data, operational metrics, or customer feedback, provides leverage because information asymmetry influences how options are evaluated. Informal credibility, the kind of trust-based influence described in Chapter 3, provides leverage because it shapes how other stakeholders interpret the negotiation and its outcomes. And the ability to slow or accelerate execution provides leverage because it determines the pace at which the transformation can actually proceed, regardless of what timelines have been formally agreed.

What makes leverage particularly dynamic in transformation contexts is that it shifts over time. Early in a program, the sponsor typically holds the greatest leverage because the initiative depends on executive commitment and resource allocation. As the program progresses, leverage migrates toward the teams responsible for implementation, because their engagement determines whether the plan translates into operational reality. As deadlines approach, the parties who control critical path activities gain leverage because delay becomes increasingly costly. And when early results emerge, the parties whose contributions produced those results gain credibility that translates into influence over subsequent decisions.

Tomás's situation illustrates this dynamic. At the program's launch, the sponsor held dominant leverage through her authority and board mandate. Six months in, the balance had shifted. The regional heads now held significant leverage because the program could not demonstrate results without their genuine participation. The regional head in Market C held a particular form of leverage: the honest inability to deliver during a leadership transition, which created a moral constraint on the program's ability to insist on the original timeline. Recognizing these shifts allowed Tomás to calibrate his approach, investing more effort in understanding the regional heads' interests and less effort in trying to invoke the sponsor's authority.

Making the Trade-Off Space Visible

One of the most practical tools for applying these concepts in preparation for a specific negotiation is a simple trade-off matrix. The structure is straightforward. Rows represent the key interests identified through the mapping process described in Chapter 5. Columns represent the possible terms or options under consideration. Cells indicate whether each option fully satisfies, partially satisfies, or fails to address each interest.

Applied to Tomás's situation, the matrix might include four interests across the rows: board-visible momentum (the sponsor's primary interest), workload manageability (Market A's primary interest), design input and evidence (Market B's primary interest), and leadership capacity (Market C's primary interest). The columns might represent three options: full simultaneous rollout in twelve months, a two-region pilot with a six-month review gate, and a staggered launch beginning with three regions and adding the remaining two after an initial stabilization period.

Laying out the matrix reveals patterns that are not obvious in conversation. The full simultaneous rollout satisfies the momentum interest completely but fails to address workload, capacity, or the desire for evidence. The two-region pilot addresses most regional concerns but creates a momentum problem with the board. The staggered launch partially satisfies every interest without fully satisfying any, which may be its strength or its weakness depending on how each party weighs partial satisfaction against the alternatives.

The value of the matrix is not that it produces the answer. It is that it makes the trade-off space visible, structured, and discussable. When Tomás can show the sponsor that a modified timeline addresses three interests that the original timeline ignores, and that ignoring those interests carries a BATNA cost of passive non-compliance, the conversation moves from positional bargaining to collaborative problem-solving. The matrix also helps identify creative options. If no existing column satisfies all interests adequately, the exercise naturally prompts the question: is there a combination of terms we have not yet considered? In Tomás's case, this led to a hybrid option, launching in three regions at nine months with dedicated transition support for Market C and a formal design review involving Market B, that was not on anyone's original list but that emerged from the visible structure of the trade-off space.

When No Agreement Is Possible

Despite the best analysis and the most creative negotiation, there are situations where no zone of possible agreement exists. The interests are genuinely incompatible. The minimum acceptable outcome for one party exceeds what the other can offer, even with issue linkage, sequencing adjustments, and the introduction of new terms. When the leader has exhausted creative options and the gap remains, the choice reduces to three alternatives.

The first is to use formal authority. A sponsor can direct compliance. A steering committee can override a regional objection. An executive can mandate a timeline. This option is always available in hierarchical organizations, and there are situations where it is the right choice, particularly when delay carries costs that exceed the costs of imposed compliance and when the decision must be made within a timeframe that does not permit further negotiation. But authority comes at a price. Directed compliance produces compliance, not commitment. The teams affected will execute the minimum required and withhold the discretionary effort that separates successful adoption from surface implementation. The trust required for future negotiations is diminished. And the organization learns that negotiation is a preliminary ritual that can be bypassed when the senior party runs out of patience, a lesson that reduces the willingness of stakeholders to engage honestly in subsequent discussions.

The second option is to restructure the problem. This means changing the scope, the timeline, the grouping of issues, or the parties involved in order to create a new configuration where agreement becomes possible. A transformation that cannot be agreed upon as a single initiative may be achievable as two sequenced phases. A budget allocation that is zero-sum across four functions may cease to be zero-sum if the timeframe is extended to allow savings from early phases to fund later ones. Restructuring requires creativity and a willingness to question whether the current framing of the problem is the only viable framing.

The third option is to accept a partial outcome and revisit the unresolved elements later. This is neither failure nor compromise in the pejorative sense. It is a recognition that some interests take time to address and that forcing resolution on every issue simultaneously can damage the agreements that have been reached on other issues. A partial agreement that preserves trust and maintains relationships is often more valuable than a comprehensive agreement that was achieved through pressure and that the losing parties feel no genuine commitment to honor.

The governing principle across all three options is this: exhaust creative alternatives before resorting to authority, and never break relationships that you will need in the next negotiation. Transformation is not a single negotiation. It is a series of negotiations that unfold over months or years, and the way any single negotiation is concluded shapes the conditions under which every subsequent conversation takes place. The leader who uses authority sparingly and visibly invests in understanding interests before invoking positional power builds a reputation that makes future negotiations easier. The leader who reaches for authority early builds a reputation that makes future negotiations harder, even when the authority is legitimate and the decision is correct.

BATNA, ZOPA, and leverage provide the analytical structure for assessing any negotiation within a transformation program. They tell the leader what each party will do if agreement fails, where the space for agreement exists, and what sources of influence shape the outcome. Combined with the interest-mapping tools from the previous chapter, they form a preparation framework that transforms negotiation from an improvised conversation into a disciplined practice. All of that analysis must ultimately be communicated. How it is framed, the language chosen, the narrative constructed around the proposed agreement, determines whether stakeholders experience it as an opportunity or a threat.

Chapter 7
Framing, Influence, and the Narratives That Move People

In the second quarter of a multi-year technology transformation at a mid-sized insurance company, two program leads were tasked with presenting the same systems migration to regional operations teams in different markets. The initiative was identical in both cases: a migration from a twenty-year-old policy administration platform to a modern cloud-based system that would standardize workflows, improve data quality, and reduce processing time. The business case had been approved at the enterprise level, and the technical requirements were the same across both regions. What differed was how each program lead chose to introduce the initiative to the teams that would carry the implementation.

The first program lead opened his presentation with a slide titled "Legacy System Replacement." He walked through the limitations of the existing platform: maintenance costs that were rising year over year, an architecture that could not support the company's digital strategy, and a growing risk of system failure as vendor support approached end-of-life. His message was factually accurate in every detail. The old system was expensive, fragile, and obsolete. The response from the room was immediate and largely negative. Questions focused on what would be lost: familiar workflows, years of customization, the institutional knowledge embedded in how the team had adapted the legacy system to local needs. The meeting ended with a list of concerns and a request for further review before any commitments were made.

The second program lead, presenting to a different regional team two weeks later, opened with a different frame. Her first slide was titled "Equipping Your Team for the Next Five Years." She acknowledged that the current system had served the company well and that the team's expertise in operating it was one of the region's strengths. She then introduced the new platform not as a replacement for something broken but as an investment in giving the team access to the tools that the highest-performing regions in the industry were already using. She described the same technical features, the same timeline, and the same resource requirements. But the conversation that followed was markedly different. Questions focused on how the transition would work, what training would look like, and when the team could begin exploring the new system's capabilities. The meeting ended with cautious interest rather than defensive resistance.

The facts presented in both meetings were the same. The difference was the frame, and that difference shaped everything that followed. The question worth examining is why framing carries such disproportionate influence over how transformation is received, how leaders can construct frames that are honest and effective, and where the line falls between influence and manipulation.

How Framing Shifts What People See

The research that explains the two meetings described above has been well established since Amos Tversky and Daniel Kahneman published their work on framing effects in the early 1980s. Their central finding was that people evaluate the same outcome differently depending on whether it is presented as a gain or a loss. When a choice is framed in terms of what will be gained, people tend to be more open to risk and more willing to act. When the same choice is framed in terms of what will be lost, they become risk-averse and protective. The effect is robust, replicable, and remarkably resistant to awareness. Even people who understand framing intellectually are influenced by it.

Applied to transformation, the implications are substantial. Every significant organizational change involves both gains and losses. A new system brings efficiency and capability but requires the abandonment of familiar tools. A restructuring creates clarity and eliminates duplication but displaces people from roles they have inhabited for years. A process standardization reduces variation and improves quality but removes the local adaptations that teams developed to fit their specific circumstances. How the leader chooses to describe the change, which elements receive emphasis, which aspects of the experience are foregrounded, and which are acknowledged but contextualized, determines whether the audience's initial response is oriented toward possibility or toward protection.

This is not merely a communication technique. It reflects a deeper reality about how humans process uncertainty. When people hear that something they value is at risk, their attention narrows to the threat. Cognitive resources are redirected toward assessing the potential loss, and the capacity to evaluate new opportunities diminishes. The first program lead's framing activated exactly this response. By leading with what was broken, he invited the room to inventory everything they stood to lose. The second program lead's framing did not deny the loss. She acknowledged the current system's value and the team's expertise. But she placed the new platform within a narrative of professional growth and competitive capability, which directed the room's attention toward what could be gained rather than what would be surrendered.

Framing also affects trust, and this dimension is easy to overlook. A frame that presents transformation as purely beneficial, that promises only upside without acknowledging difficulty, feels dishonest to people who know from experience that organizational change always involves cost. The audience may not articulate this feeling as distrust, but it manifests as skepticism, heightened scrutiny of the details, and a reluctance to commit. A frame that acknowledges the difficulty honestly while articulating a compelling reason to proceed despite that difficulty builds credibility precisely because it treats the audience as adults who can handle complexity. The second program lead earned trust not by minimizing the challenge but by respecting the team's intelligence enough to present it within a narrative that made the challenge feel purposeful.

Identity: The Deepest Layer of Framing

Of all the framing challenges that arise in transformation, the most consequential involve professional identity. People do not merely perform roles within organizations. They construct meaning from those roles. A procurement specialist who has spent fifteen years developing expertise in supplier negotiation does not simply execute a function. She has built a professional identity around that expertise, and her sense of competence, value, and belonging is intertwined with it. When a transformation introduces an automated sourcing platform that reduces the need for manual negotiation, the business case may be compelling. But the message received by the specialist is not only operational. It is personal. It says, or can be heard to say, that the work she has defined herself by is no longer necessary.

This dynamic explains why some of the most intense resistance in transformation programs comes from the people who are most skilled in the current way of working. Their competence is precisely what is being made obsolete, and the more deeply that competence is tied to their identity, the more threatening the change feels. A narrative that says "your old way of working is being replaced" attacks identity directly, even when the replacement is objectively superior. It tells the individual that the thing they were good at no longer matters.

Constructing narratives that protect identity while still advancing the transformation requires a different kind of honesty. The frame must acknowledge the value of existing expertise and position it as an asset in the transition rather than a casualty of it. "Your understanding of supplier dynamics is exactly what we need to configure the new platform effectively. The system handles the transactional work, but it cannot replicate the judgment you bring to complex negotiations." This kind of framing is not flattery. It is an accurate recognition that domain expertise remains valuable even when the tools change, and it gives the individual a bridge between who they have been and who they are being asked to become. The difference between a narrative that provokes resistance and one that enables engagement is often not a difference in content but a difference in whether the narrative allows people to carry their professional identity forward into the new environment or requires them to leave it behind.

Framing in Practice: Common Scenarios

Framing challenges recur across transformation types, and certain patterns appear with enough regularity that leaders can prepare for them in advance. The following table presents the most common scenarios, showing the typical frame that generates resistance alongside an alternative that addresses the same reality more effectively.

Table 9.

Framing Choices in Common Transformation Scenarios

Scenario	Typical Frame	Why It Fails	More Effective Frame	Why It Works
Cost Reduction Program	"We need to reduce costs by 15% across all functions."	Activates loss aversion. Teams hear "cuts" and immediately focus on what will be taken away. Defensive behavior begins before any conversation about how the reductions will be achieved.	"We are freeing up resources to invest in the capabilities that will drive growth over the next three years. Each function will play a role in identifying where current spending can be redirected toward higher-value work."	Reframes the same financial target as a purposeful reallocation rather than a subtraction. Gives teams agency in the process and connects the effort to a future they can participate in shaping.
Compliance or Regulatory Initiative	"New regulations require us to change how we operate. Failure to comply carries significant penalties."	Frames the initiative as an externally imposed obligation with no upside. People comply minimally because the motivation is avoidance of punishment rather than achievement of a positive outcome.	"The regulatory landscape is shifting in ways that create an opportunity to strengthen how we manage risk and build trust with our clients and regulators. Meeting the new standards positions us ahead of competitors who will struggle to adapt."	Transforms an obligation into a competitive advantage. Engages professional pride and positions the team's work as forward-looking rather than reactive.
Technology Adoption	"We are replacing the legacy system, which is outdated and no longer supported."	Defines the change in terms of what is being taken away. Teams who built expertise on the legacy system hear that their skills are obsolete.	"We are giving your team access to the tools that leading organizations in our industry are using. Your experience with the current system makes you uniquely qualified to shape how the new platform is configured for our needs."	Preserves identity by positioning existing expertise as an asset. Creates a role for the team in the transition rather than a passive experience of being transitioned.
Organizational Restructuring	"We are eliminating redundancies and streamlining the organization."	The word "eliminating" produces anxiety even among people whose roles are secure. "Redundancies" implies that some people's work was unnecessary.	"We are reorganizing to create clearer accountability and stronger collaboration across teams. This means some roles will evolve, and we will work with each affected team to ensure the transition is handled with care."	Acknowledges impact honestly while framing the purpose positively. The commitment to work with affected teams signals respect and reduces the fear of being treated as a line item.
Process Standardization	"All regions will adopt the global standard process. Local variations will be phased out."	Frames standardization as the removal of something (local adaptation) rather than the addition of something. Regions hear that their way of working has been judged inferior.	"We are building a common foundation that every region can build on. The global standard creates consistency where it matters most, and we will work with each region to ensure that local requirements are reflected in how the standard is applied."	Preserves regional identity by acknowledging local expertise. Positions the standard as a foundation rather than a replacement, leaving room for legitimate adaptation within a shared framework.

Influence as a Practical Discipline

Framing shapes how a message is received. Influence shapes whether the message leads to action. The two are related but distinct. A well-framed narrative can open the door to engagement, but converting that engagement into committed participation often requires the application of broader influence principles that operate alongside rational analysis.

Robert Cialdini's research identified six principles of influence that have proven remarkably consistent across settings, and each has direct application in transformation work. Rather than cataloguing them as an academic exercise, the following treatment focuses on how each principle functions as a practical tool inside organizations.

Reciprocity operates on the principle that people feel obligated to return what they receive. In transformation contexts, this means that giving something of value before asking for commitment creates a psychological foundation for cooperation. Providing a team with additional resources, early access to information, or visible support during a difficult period creates goodwill that makes subsequent requests for engagement feel like a natural extension of the relationship rather than an imposition. The investment must be genuine. Calculated generosity is transparent and produces cynicism rather than reciprocity.

Consistency reflects the human tendency to act in alignment with prior commitments and stated values. When a stakeholder has publicly endorsed a principle, such as the importance of operational excellence or the value of innovation, linking the transformation to that principle makes resistance psychologically uncomfortable. The leader is not pressuring the stakeholder to change. She is inviting them to act consistently with what they have already said they believe. This works best when the connection is genuine rather than rhetorical. A forced link between a stated value and a specific program demand will feel manipulative. A natural connection will feel like a reminder of shared purpose.

Social proof is the tendency to look to others when deciding how to behave in ambiguous situations. During transformation, when uncertainty is high and the right course of action is unclear, people look to respected peers for guidance. This is why early adoption by a credible team carries influence far beyond its operational significance. When a respected regional head commits publicly to the new operating model, other regional heads recalculate their own positions. The change leader who understands social proof invests in securing early commitments from the most credible and visible stakeholders, not because those commitments are operationally necessary in the first phase, but because they shift the interpretive frame for everyone else.

Authority in this context does not mean hierarchical power. It means the credibility of the messenger. The same message delivered by a trusted technical expert carries more weight than the same message delivered by a program manager the audience does not know. Choosing the right messenger for each audience, matching the speaker's credibility to the audience's concerns, is one of the most underutilized influence tools in transformation work. A clinical director speaking to medical staff about a new system carries authority that no project manager can replicate. A peer who has already navigated the transition successfully carries authority that no executive sponsor can match.

Liking reflects the reality that people are more receptive to influence from individuals they know, respect, and feel connected to. In transformation, this means that the quality of the relationship between the change leader and the stakeholder matters as much as the quality of the argument. Investing in genuine relationships, not transactional networking but authentic engagement with the stakeholder's perspective, builds the relational capital that makes difficult conversations productive rather than adversarial.

Scarcity creates urgency by highlighting what is available only for a limited time or under specific conditions. In transformation, leaders can use genuine scarcity honestly: early adopters may receive additional support that will not be available later, or the window for influencing the design of a new process may close once specifications are finalized. The key constraint is honesty. Artificial scarcity, manufactured deadlines, or exaggerated consequences corrode trust and teach stakeholders to discount future urgency signals.

The Line Between Influence and Manipulation

The tools described in this chapter are powerful, and their power creates a responsibility that deserves explicit attention. The line between influence and manipulation is not always easy to locate, but its essential characteristic is clear: influence respects autonomy and operates through honest information, while manipulation subverts autonomy through deception, omission, or coercion.

In practice, this distinction rests on several principles. The framing must be honest. Presenting a cost reduction as an investment in future capability is legitimate if the savings genuinely will be reinvested. It crosses the line if the reinvestment claim is fiction designed to reduce resistance to cuts that have no offsetting benefit. The information provided must be complete enough for the audience to make an informed judgment. Omitting material facts that would change the stakeholder's assessment of the situation is manipulation, even if nothing stated is technically false. The promises made must be keepable. Committing to additional support, design input, or protected timelines in order to secure agreement, and then failing to deliver, destroys trust in a way that extends far beyond the current negotiation. It teaches the organization that agreements reached through negotiation are unreliable, and that lesson makes every subsequent change harder.

The long-term cost of manipulative framing is severe and compounding. Organizations have memories. People who felt deceived by the framing of one transformation carry that experience into their response to the next. They become harder to engage, more skeptical of reassurances, and more reliant on their own protective strategies. The change leader who frames honestly and influences ethically, acknowledging difficulty, respecting intelligence, and delivering on commitments, builds a reputation that makes each subsequent negotiation easier. In a context where transformation is continuous rather than episodic, this reputational capital is one of the most valuable assets a leader can accumulate.

The concepts developed in the first seven chapters of this book, from the foundations of alignment through the skills of interest identification, mapping, leverage analysis, and framing, provide the toolkit for navigating the human dynamics of transformation. Part III turns to the deeper patterns that shape those dynamics: the behavioral biases that make rational plans meet irrational resistance, the game-theoretic structures that trap organizations in inefficient equilibria, and the strategic choreography required when multiple parties, multiple interests, and multiple negotiations must be managed simultaneously.

PART III
BEHAVIORAL SCIENCE AND STRATEGIC DYNAMICS

Chapter 8

Behavioral Bias in Change: Why Rational Plans Meet Irrational Resistance

The shared services consolidation at a European manufacturing company was, by any analytical standard, a well-designed program. The business case showed a 22% reduction in transaction processing costs within two years, supported by benchmarking data from three comparable companies that had completed similar transitions. The implementation plan was realistic, with a phased timeline that allowed each function to transition at a pace calibrated to its operational cycle. The executive committee had approved the initiative unanimously, and the program team included experienced practitioners who had delivered shared services models before. When the plan was presented to the finance operations teams whose work would be most directly affected, the presentation was clear, the data was solid, and the questions that followed were answered with specificity and patience.

Three months later, the program was behind schedule in every function except one. The finance operations teams had attended every workshop, completed every required assessment, and participated in every governance meeting. They had also, almost without exception, continued to perform their work exactly as they had before the program began. New procedures documented in the transition plan were acknowledged but not adopted. Workarounds that the new model was designed to eliminate remained in daily use. When asked about progress, team leads referenced ongoing dependencies, unresolved questions, and the need for additional clarity before they could commit to the new workflows. Nothing was refused. Nothing was visibly obstructed. But the behavioral change that the business case depended on had not occurred.

The program director, reviewing the situation at the quarterly checkpoint, described the gap to her sponsor in a way that many transformation leaders will recognize: "The plan is right. The people aren't moving." This formulation, which treats the plan as the fixed reference point and human behavior as the variable that needs correction, contains the precise error that this chapter addresses. The plan was designed through rational analysis. It was received by human beings whose responses to change are governed not only by rational evaluation but by a set of predictable psychological patterns that operate below the level of conscious deliberation. The resistance that the program encountered was not irrational. It was entirely predictable. The problem was that the program design had not accounted for how people actually process the experience of being asked to change.

The Weight of What Already Exists

The most pervasive bias affecting transformation is the one that requires the least dramatic trigger to activate. Status quo bias describes the tendency for people to prefer the current state of affairs simply because it is current. This preference is not merely habitual. It is psychologically reinforced by a related mechanism, loss aversion, which causes people to weight potential losses more heavily than equivalent potential gains. The combination of these two forces creates a powerful inertia that operates independently of the objective merits of the proposed change.

In practical terms, this means that a process which has "always worked," even one that is visibly inefficient, carries psychological value that the business case does not capture. The familiar process is known. Its limitations are understood and have been compensated for through workarounds that the team has developed over time. The risks associated with it have been absorbed into the team's operating rhythm. By contrast, the proposed replacement, however superior in design, introduces a period of uncertainty during which the familiar compensatory mechanisms no longer apply and new ones have not yet developed. The rational calculation may clearly favor the new process. The psychological calculation, which weighs the certain loss of the familiar against the uncertain gain of the new, often does not.

Loss aversion intensifies this pattern. Research consistently shows that the psychological impact of losing something is roughly twice as powerful as the impact of gaining something of equivalent value. When a transformation asks people to give up established workflows, familiar tools, or proven methods of managing their responsibilities, the perceived loss registers with greater psychological force than the promised improvement. This is why a business case showing a 22% cost reduction can fail to motivate teams whose daily experience of the change is not "gaining efficiency" but "losing the way I know how to do my job."

Arguing harder for the merits of the change is not the answer. The people experiencing these biases are not failing to understand the business case. They are processing it through a psychological system that assigns disproportionate weight to what is being given up. Effective design reduces the perceived magnitude of the loss by making the first step small and reversible, by preserving as much of the familiar environment as possible during early phases, and by ensuring that the transition does not require people to abandon their current competencies before they have developed confidence in new ones. A phased approach is not just an operational convenience. It is a psychological necessity that gives the bias time to recalibrate as the new state gradually becomes the new status quo.

When Change Threatens Who You Are

Status quo bias operates at the level of routines and habits. Identity threat operates at a deeper level, one that affects how people understand their professional worth. When a transformation alters someone's role, displaces their expertise, or diminishes the standing they have built within the organization, the response is not simply reluctance to change a process. It is a defense of the self.

This dynamic was explored in Chapter 7 in the context of framing, but the psychological mechanism deserves fuller treatment here. Identity threat triggers defensive behavior that often appears rational on the surface. A leader whose authority is reduced by a new governance model may argue against it on the basis of operational efficiency. A specialist whose expertise is being replaced by technology may raise legitimate concerns about risk and quality. These arguments are not dishonest. The individuals raising them may genuinely believe in their validity. But the intensity and persistence of the objections, the fact that they continue even after the rational concerns have been addressed, signals that something beyond operational analysis is at stake.

Loss of control compounds the effect. The experience of having decisions made about your work without your involvement produces a psychological response that is distinct from disagreement with the decision itself. People who intellectually support a change may still resist it if they feel that the process excluded them, that their perspective was not sought, or that the decision was presented as settled before they had the opportunity to influence it. This is not mere ego. It reflects a legitimate psychological need for agency, the sense that one has meaningful input into the conditions of one's own professional life.

The practical implications point toward involvement rather than communication. Telling people about a change, even telling them well, does not satisfy the need for agency. Involving them in shaping the change, even within constrained parameters, does. This does not mean that every decision must be made by consensus. It means that the people most affected by a decision should have a genuine opportunity to influence how it is implemented, and that this opportunity should be offered before the sense of exclusion has produced defensive reactions that are difficult to reverse.

The Drift from Caution to Conviction

Confirmation bias describes the tendency to seek, interpret, and remember information in ways that confirm existing beliefs. In transformation contexts, this bias has a particularly corrosive effect because it operates progressively. An initial interpretation, once formed, becomes self-reinforcing over time as the individual selectively attends to evidence that supports it and discounts evidence that contradicts it.

Consider how this plays out in practice. A team member who forms an early impression that the transformation is poorly managed will notice every missed deadline, every unclear communication, and every instance of inconsistency between what was promised and what was delivered. Positive developments, successful pilots, resolved concerns, adjusted plans that reflect feedback, will receive less attention or will be reinterpreted through the negative frame: "They're only doing that because they know it's going badly." Over weeks and months, the initial caution hardens into settled conviction without any single event that justifies the shift. The individual's position has drifted from reasonable skepticism to entrenched opposition, and they will sincerely believe that their view is based on evidence.

Assumption drift, the gradual hardening of initial impressions into fixed beliefs, is confirmation bias operating over time. It explains why early experiences in a transformation carry disproportionate weight. The first workshop, the first status update, the first interaction between the program team and the affected stakeholders, establishes the interpretive frame through which all subsequent information is filtered. A disorganized first workshop produces a frame of incompetence that may survive months of subsequent competence. A dismissive response to an early concern produces a frame of indifference that may persist long after the concern has been addressed.

The practical response operates on two fronts. The first is to invest disproportionately in getting early experiences right. The first touchpoint between the transformation program and each stakeholder group should be designed with the same care that a company brings to a product launch, because it establishes the perceptual frame through which everything that follows will be evaluated. The second front is subtler: introducing disconfirming evidence in ways that do not trigger defensiveness. Directly telling someone that their interpretation is wrong activates a different bias, the backfire effect, where challenged beliefs are held more tightly rather than less. More effective approaches include creating direct experiences that contradict the existing interpretation without explicitly labeling them as counterevidence, inviting skeptics into problem-solving roles where they encounter positive information through their own investigation rather than through persuasion, and using respected peers rather than program officials to share observations that conflict with the negative frame.

Emotional Responses as Information

Transformation literature frequently treats emotional reactions to change as obstacles that must be managed or overcome. This framing contains a fundamental error. Emotions are not the opposite of rationality. They are a parallel processing system that carries information about what people value, what they fear, and what they interpret as threatening or promising. A team member who responds to a restructuring announcement with visible anxiety is not being irrational. She is processing information about her professional security through an emotional system that operates faster and with different priorities than analytical thought.

The mistake that leaders most commonly make with emotional responses is to counter them with logic. Presenting data to someone who is frightened does not reduce the fear. It communicates that the speaker has not understood what is actually happening in the conversation. The data answers a question that the individual is not asking. Her question is not "Is this change justified?" but "Am I going to be okay?" These are fundamentally different questions, and they require fundamentally different responses.

Effective engagement with emotional responses follows a sequence that begins with acknowledgment rather than argument. Acknowledging the emotional reality of a situation, saying in effect "I understand this is difficult and your concern makes sense given what you're facing," does not concede the argument or abandon the program's objectives. It establishes that the leader is responding to the actual experience of the person in front of them rather than to a simplified version of that experience that is more convenient to address. Validation follows acknowledgment: confirming that the concerns are legitimate even when the conclusion drawn from them may not be. Only after the emotional reality has been recognized does reframing become possible, because only then has the leader earned the standing to offer a different perspective on the situation. This sequence, acknowledgment followed by validation followed by reframing, is not a technique. It is a reflection of how trust is built in conversations where emotional stakes are high.

Recognition and Response: A Practical Reference

The biases described in this chapter are not obscure psychological phenomena. They are everyday realities that transformation leaders encounter in nearly every significant conversation. The following table compresses the key patterns into a reference format designed for practical use: what to watch for, what the behavior reveals about the underlying psychological mechanism, and what adjustments to design and communication can address it.

Table 10.

Behavioral Biases in Transformation: Recognition and Response

Bias	How It Manifests	What It Means	Practical Response
Status Quo Bias	Preference for existing processes even when alternatives are demonstrably superior; reluctance to abandon familiar tools; continued use of workarounds after new processes are introduced.	The current state carries psychological value simply because it is known and its risks are understood. Change introduces uncertainty that feels heavier than the inefficiency it replaces.	Make the first step small and reversible. Preserve familiar elements where possible during early phases. Allow new and old approaches to coexist temporarily so the transition feels gradual rather than abrupt.
Loss Aversion	Disproportionate focus on what will be lost rather than what will be gained; stronger emotional response to potential losses than to equivalent potential gains; reluctance to commit despite favorable analysis.	Losses register with roughly twice the psychological force of equivalent gains. The business case may be compelling, but the experienced reality foregrounds what is being surrendered.	Frame the change in terms of what is being gained or protected rather than what is being replaced. Ensure that early experiences of the change deliver tangible, visible benefits before demanding full commitment.
Identity Threat	Defensive objections that persist after operational concerns are addressed; resistance concentrated among the most skilled practitioners of the current approach; arguments that reframe the change as unnecessary rather than unworkable.	The change threatens the professional identity, standing, or sense of competence that the individual has built. The resistance is not about the process but about what the process means for who they are.	Position existing expertise as essential to the transition. Create roles that carry forward the value of current knowledge. Ensure the narrative acknowledges what the individual has contributed, not only what the organization needs next.
Loss of Control	Resistance even from intellectually supportive individuals; focus on process objections rather than substance; demands for more information, more review, or more time before committing.	The individual feels excluded from decisions that affect their professional life. The need for agency has not been met, and resistance is a way of reclaiming influence over the process.	Involve affected individuals in shaping implementation before announcing decisions. Provide genuine opportunities for input within defined parameters. Distinguish between decisions that are fixed and decisions that remain open to influence.
Confirmation Bias	Selective attention to negative signals; dismissal or reinterpretation of positive evidence; progressive hardening of initial skepticism without new justifying events.	An early interpretation has become self-reinforcing. The individual is not ignoring evidence but is processing it through a frame that filters for confirmation of existing beliefs.	Invest heavily in early positive experiences. Introduce disconfirming evidence through direct experience and trusted peers rather than through argument. Create opportunities for skeptics to discover contradictory evidence through their own engagement.
Emotional Reactivity	Visible anxiety, frustration, or withdrawal that is disproportionate to the operational implications of the change; difficulty engaging with analytical content during discussions of the transformation.	Emotional processing is operating faster and with higher priority than analytical assessment. The individual is responding to what the change means for their security, identity, or relationships, not to the change itself.	Begin with acknowledgment and validation rather than data and logic. Address the emotional reality before attempting to reframe the situation. Earn the right to offer a different perspective by first demonstrating understanding of the current experience.

These biases rarely operate one at a time. In most transformation situations, several are active simultaneously, reinforcing each other in ways that amplify resistance beyond what any single bias would produce on its own. A team experiencing status quo bias, loss aversion, and confirmation bias simultaneously is not three times as resistant as a team experiencing one. The combination creates a qualitatively different kind of inertia, where the effort required to shift the pattern must address multiple psychological mechanisms at once. This is why isolated interventions, a better presentation, a stronger business case, a more forceful mandate, rarely succeed. Effective response requires understanding the full psychological landscape and designing an approach that works with its contours rather than against them.

A different kind of pattern runs alongside the individual biases described here: the strategic dynamics that emerge when groups of rational individuals, each acting in their own interest, produce collectively inefficient outcomes. Game theory provides the lens for understanding those dynamics and designing interventions that shift the equilibrium toward cooperation.

Chapter 9
Game Theory for Change Leaders

The data governance initiative at a global professional services firm had a straightforward objective: bring client engagement data from three major practice areas onto a shared analytics platform so that cross-selling opportunities, resource allocation patterns, and client risk concentrations could be assessed at the enterprise level. The business case was approved without significant objection. Each of the three practice heads acknowledged, publicly and in writing, that the integrated view would benefit the firm and their own teams. A shared platform was provisioned. Migration protocols were designed. A timeline was agreed. All that remained was for each practice area to contribute its data.

Twelve months later, the platform was still empty.

The pattern that produced this outcome was not complicated, but it was invisible to anyone approaching the situation as a communication or change management problem. Each practice area held data that reflected its performance in granular detail: client profitability, utilization rates, engagement duration, and partner productivity. Contributing this data to a shared platform meant making that performance visible to the other two practices and to firm leadership. In isolation, this transparency was manageable. But the value of contributing depended entirely on whether the others contributed as well. If all three practices shared their data simultaneously, the result would be a genuinely useful enterprise view. If one practice contributed while the others waited, the contributing practice would have exposed its performance data with no reciprocal visibility into the others. The rational response to this structure, for each practice independently, was to wait.

And so each waited. Status updates reported progress on technical preparation. Governance meetings discussed data quality standards. Working groups refined metadata definitions. All of this activity was genuine, but none of it involved actually contributing data to the platform. Each practice area was performing readiness while deferring the act that carried risk. The initiative had not been rejected. It had been trapped by a structure that made caution the individually rational choice for every party involved.

Game theory, the study of strategic decision-making among interdependent actors, provides a set of concepts that explain why groups of intelligent, well-intentioned people produce collectively irrational results. These are not academic abstractions. They describe situations that transformation leaders encounter with remarkable frequency: teams that would all benefit from cooperation but cannot find a way to begin, behaviors that persist despite being visibly inefficient, and incentive structures that inadvertently reward the very patterns the transformation is designed to eliminate.

Why Inefficient Behaviors Persist

The concept of Nash equilibrium, named after mathematician John Nash, describes a situation in which no individual participant can improve their outcome by changing their behavior alone, given what they expect the other participants to do. In such a state, even if the collective result is suboptimal, the system remains stable because no single party has a rational reason to move.

This concept illuminates a pattern that transformation leaders find endlessly frustrating: behaviors that everyone acknowledges are inefficient but that no one changes. A common example involves reporting processes. Multiple teams may maintain separate reporting systems that produce overlapping outputs, consume duplicated effort, and generate inconsistent data. Everyone agrees that a consolidated reporting model would be better. Yet no team moves to adopt one, because the transition cost falls entirely on the team that moves first while the benefits depend on others following. Each team's current behavior, maintaining its own system, represents the best response to the expectation that others will do the same. The equilibrium holds.

The insight for transformation leaders is fundamental: when resistance takes this form, the problem is not the people. It is the structure. Persuading individual teams to change their behavior will not work if the structural incentives continue to reward the existing pattern. The leader who responds to this kind of stalemate with better communication, stronger arguments for the business case, or more emphatic expressions of executive support is addressing a structural problem with interpersonal tools. The solution requires changing the structure so that a different set of behaviors becomes the individually rational choice.

The Dilemma of Going First

The data governance scenario at the professional services firm is a variant of what game theory calls the prisoner's dilemma: a situation where mutual cooperation produces the best collective outcome, but where each party has an individual incentive to defect, to withhold cooperation while hoping that others will cooperate, because being the sole cooperator produces the worst individual outcome.

In transformation contexts, this dilemma appears whenever the value of participation depends on the participation of others. Shared service consolidations require each function to transfer work to a central unit, but the function that transfers first bears the transition cost while retaining full accountability for outcomes during a period when the central unit has not yet proven its capability. Legacy system sunsets require teams to abandon familiar tools and adopt new ones, but the team that migrates first loses access to established workarounds while the teams that wait continue to benefit from the old system's predictability. Data transparency initiatives, as the opening example illustrates, require teams to expose their performance to scrutiny, but the team that shares first bears the vulnerability while others retain their informational advantage.

In each case, the rational individual response is to wait, to let someone else absorb the cost of going first, and to commit only after the risks have been demonstrated to be manageable. The collective result is paralysis.

The classical prisoner's dilemma, as a one-time interaction between two parties, has no cooperative solution. Each party's dominant strategy is to defect regardless of what the other does. But transformation does not take place in a single interaction. It unfolds over months and years, through repeated encounters between the same parties. This changes the calculus fundamentally. In repeated interactions, strategies based on conditional cooperation become viable. A party can commit to cooperating as long as others reciprocate, and can withdraw cooperation if others fail to follow through. This possibility, combined with the reputational consequences of being seen as the party that refused to participate, creates conditions where cooperation can emerge if the leader structures the interaction appropriately.

The practical mechanisms for enabling this emergence are well established. Transparency is the first requirement: each party must be able to observe whether others are cooperating or defecting. When contributions to a shared platform are tracked and visible, the social cost of non-participation increases. Credible commitments are the second: agreements that carry consequences for non-compliance shift the calculus by making defection costly rather than cost-free. A governance decision that ties a practice area's access to enterprise analytics to its own data contribution, for example, creates a link between cooperation and benefit that the voluntary structure lacked. Simultaneity is the third: structuring the interaction so that all parties act at the same time, or within a narrow window, eliminates the vulnerability of going first. The data governance initiative could have required all three practice areas to contribute an initial dataset on the same date, reviewed jointly, rather than leaving the sequence to individual discretion.

Breaking the Coordination Trap

Coordination failures represent a related but distinct pattern. Where the prisoner's dilemma involves a tension between individual and collective interest, coordination failures involve situations where all parties share the same interest but cannot synchronize their actions to achieve it. Everyone wants to cooperate, but no one can move without confidence that others will move simultaneously.

The distinction matters because coordination failures look like resistance but are actually the rational response to uncertainty about others' behavior. A team that would happily adopt a new process if it knew that its peer teams were doing the same will hesitate if that assurance is absent, not because it opposes the change but because unilateral adoption creates risk without guaranteed collective benefit. Leaders often misinterpret this inertia as reluctance, responding with stronger messaging and escalated mandates that address a motivational problem that does not exist.

Breaking coordination failures requires reducing the uncertainty that prevents synchronized action. Four approaches have proven effective across a range of transformation contexts.

Creating visible first-movers addresses the uncertainty directly. When a respected team commits publicly to the change and its experience is made visible to others, the uncertainty about what adoption looks like and what it costs begins to resolve. Pilot programs serve this function not only as operational tests but as social proof that the change is survivable and potentially beneficial. The visibility is critical. A pilot whose results are shared in a governance forum and discussed openly reduces uncertainty far more effectively than a pilot whose results are communicated through a written report that may or may not be read.

Establishing credible commitments changes the calculus by making non-participation costly. When all parties sign a binding agreement with defined consequences for non-compliance, the uncertainty about others' behavior diminishes because the cost of defection has been raised. The commitment must be genuinely binding. A governance decision that is understood to be revisable or unenforceable does not reduce uncertainty. It merely adds another layer of performative alignment.

Reducing the cost of going first protects early adopters from the vulnerability that makes waiting the rational choice. This might take the form of additional resources during the transition period, a temporary relaxation of performance metrics, or a public commitment from leadership that early adopters will not be penalized for the disruptions that inevitably accompany any significant process change. When the cost of going first is visibly reduced, the calculus shifts and the coordination barrier weakens.

Building sequential momentum combines elements of all three approaches. Rather than attempting to coordinate all parties simultaneously, the leader negotiates a small coalition of willing first-movers into alignment, ensures that their experience is positive and visible, and then uses that evidence to bring the next group into the fold. Each successful round of adoption reduces the uncertainty for the next group, and the social proof accumulated by the growing coalition creates its own pressure for participation. This approach is slower than a simultaneous launch but far more reliable in contexts where the coordination barrier is high.

Redesigning the Incentive Landscape

The deepest application of game theory to transformation involves not managing individual negotiations but redesigning the incentive structures that determine which behaviors are rational in the first place. When the existing incentive landscape rewards behaviors that conflict with the transformation's objectives, no amount of negotiation skill will produce lasting alignment. The equilibrium will reassert itself as soon as attention shifts elsewhere.

The principle is deceptively simple: make cooperation the easy path, not the heroic one. In practice, this requires examining how rewards, metrics, accountability mechanisms, and recognition systems interact with the behaviors the transformation requires.

Shared metrics are among the most powerful tools available. When two teams that need to collaborate are measured exclusively on their individual performance, their rational focus is internal. Each will optimize for its own metrics even at the expense of the joint outcome. Introducing a shared metric, one that both teams are accountable for and that can only be achieved through collaboration, restructures the incentive so that cooperation becomes individually rational. The metric must be meaningful. A token shared metric that carries no real consequences will be treated as what it is: a symbolic gesture that does not actually change the calculus.

Joint accountability operates on a similar principle. When accountability for a transformation milestone rests with a single team, that team bears the full weight of failure while other teams that contributed to the outcome bear none. Distributing accountability across the teams whose collective effort determines success creates an incentive structure where each team has a stake in the performance of the others, which in turn creates a rational basis for mutual support rather than mutual indifference.

Visible consequences for non-participation address the free-rider problem that undermines many transformation initiatives. When there is no meaningful difference between full participation and minimal compliance, the rational strategy is minimal compliance. Introducing visible consequences, not punitive measures but transparent distinctions in how participants and non-participants are treated in terms of resources, recognition, or access to future opportunities, shifts the equilibrium by making cooperation visibly rewarded and non-participation visibly costly.

Recognition that values collective contribution addresses the subtler dimension of incentive design. In most organizations, recognition systems celebrate individual achievement: the leader who delivered a result, the team that met a target, the function that exceeded expectations. During transformation, the behaviors that matter most are often collaborative: the team that shared resources with a struggling peer, the leader who modified her timeline to accommodate a cross-functional dependency, the function that absorbed short-term cost to enable a collective benefit. When these contributions are recognized publicly and consistently, the signal to the organization is that cooperation is valued and observed, which changes the social incentive alongside the structural one.

Two Patterns in Practice

The dynamics described in this chapter become most visible in extended examples where the equilibrium, the incentive structure, and the intervention can all be traced.

In a global insurance company undertaking a claims processing standardization, four regional offices were asked to migrate from their local systems to a single enterprise platform. Each office's processing metrics were tied to its regional performance scorecard, and each office had spent years optimizing its local system to meet those regional targets. The enterprise platform would eventually produce better outcomes, but the transition period would temporarily depress processing speed, which would affect each region's scorecard. No region wanted to be the first to absorb that temporary performance hit. The result was a twelve-month period during which all four regions expressed support for the initiative and none began migration. The equilibrium broke only when the program team, recognizing the game-theoretic structure of the problem, negotiated three changes simultaneously. First, regional performance metrics were adjusted during the migration window to exclude processing speed from the scorecard, reducing the cost of going first. Second, a shared metric was introduced that measured each region's contribution to the enterprise migration, creating positive visibility for early movers. Third, the first two regions to volunteer were offered additional technical support during their transition, making their experience visibly easier than it would otherwise have been. Within two months of these changes, all four regions had committed to migration timelines, and two had begun active implementation.

In a technology company consolidating three engineering teams under a shared services model, the coordination failure took a different form. Each team was willing to contribute engineers to the shared pool but wanted to retain its most experienced specialists for local projects. The result was that each team offered its least utilized staff, which produced a shared services unit perceived as a repository for underperformers rather than a center of excellence. The equilibrium was inefficient, it produced a weak shared service that failed to deliver value, which in turn justified the teams' reluctance to contribute their best talent, but it was stable because no individual team could improve its outcome by contributing more while others contributed less. The intervention involved restructuring the model so that participation in the shared service was rotational rather than permanent, with each team's top performers serving six-month assignments before returning to their home team. This eliminated the fear of permanently losing key staff. It was combined with a recognition mechanism that treated shared service assignments as career-enhancing leadership experiences rather than as lateral diversions. The result was a qualitative transformation in the caliber of contributions, which improved the shared service's output, which in turn justified further investment, creating a virtuous cycle that replaced the previous equilibrium trap.

Table 11.

Common Game-Theoretic Patterns in Transformation

Pattern	How It Manifests	Underlying Strategic Logic	Intervention Approach
Coordination Failure	All parties support the change but none moves first; initiative stalls despite unanimous formal endorsement.	Each party's optimal action depends on what others do; uncertainty about others' behavior makes waiting the individually rational choice.	Create visible first-movers; establish credible simultaneous commitments; reduce the cost of going first; build sequential momentum through pilot success.
Prisoner's Dilemma / Free-Rider Problem	Teams withhold data, resources, or commitment while hoping others contribute first; participation is minimal despite stated support.	Contributing creates short-term vulnerability with no guaranteed reciprocation; defection is the dominant strategy in a single interaction.	Increase transparency so contributions are visible; introduce reciprocal structures; link benefits to participation; create binding commitments with consequences.
Equilibrium Trap	Inefficient behaviors persist despite universal recognition that they are suboptimal; each party acts rationally given what others are doing.	No individual party can improve its outcome by changing alone; the collective inefficiency is stable because unilateral change is costly.	Change the structure rather than persuading individuals; introduce shared metrics, joint accountability, or altered incentive systems that make a different set of behaviors individually rational.
Escalation Spiral	Competing teams increase investment in conflicting approaches, each justifying its position by the other's escalation.	Each party responds rationally to the other's behavior, producing an arms race dynamic that consumes resources without resolving the underlying conflict.	Introduce a decision mechanism that resolves the conflict structurally; create a superordinate goal that reframes the competition as collaboration; use authority to set boundaries if the spiral threatens program integrity.

The value of game theory for transformation leaders lies not in its mathematical formalism but in its clarity about structure. When resistance appears to be motivational, asking "What game are these people playing?" often reveals that the problem is structural: the incentive landscape makes non-cooperation rational, the coordination mechanism is absent, or the equilibrium rewards precisely the behaviors the transformation seeks to change. Recognizing these patterns shifts the leader's focus from persuasion to design, from changing minds to changing the conditions under which minds operate. The most complex application of that structural perspective is managing multiple parties, multiple interests, and multiple interdependent agreements simultaneously.

Chapter 10
Sequencing, Coalitions, and Multi-Party Negotiation

The steering committee meeting was scheduled for Thursday at two o'clock. Eight people would be in the room: the executive sponsor, four functional heads whose teams were directly affected by the proposed changes to the company's global procurement operating model, the head of IT who controlled the platform budget, the HR director whose team would manage the workforce implications, and the change leader herself, a program director named Adriana who had been managing the initiative for seven months.

On paper, the meeting's purpose was to approve the transition plan for the second phase of the program: the consolidation of category management activities from regional teams into three specialized hubs. The plan had been developed over several weeks, reviewed by the program team, and circulated in advance. What the agenda did not capture, and what no written document could capture, was that the meeting would succeed or fail based on conversations that had not yet happened.

Adriana understood this. She had learned, through experience that included several painful early-career lessons, that a steering committee meeting is not where alignment is created. It is where alignment is confirmed or, when preparation has been insufficient, where its absence becomes visible in ways that are difficult to repair. The actual negotiation happens before the meeting, in a series of bilateral conversations where individual interests are explored, concerns are surfaced, proposals are tested, and the conditions for productive group discussion are established. By the time the group convenes, the leader should know what each participant thinks, what each needs, and where the potential points of agreement and friction lie. The meeting itself should contain no surprises.

She opened her notebook and began mapping the sequence. Who needed to be spoken with first, and why. What each conversation needed to accomplish. How the outcome of one conversation would shape the possibilities for the next. The order was not arbitrary. It was strategic, and getting it right would determine whether Thursday's meeting produced a decision or produced another round of the cautious deferral that had slowed the program's first phase.

Complex transformations involve not a single negotiation but many, conducted across multiple parties in a specific order, with results that cascade from one conversation into the next. The choreography of that process, who is engaged when, what is discussed at each stage, and how early agreements create momentum or constraints for later ones, is a leadership skill that is rarely taught and frequently decisive.

Why the Order Changes the Outcome

The temptation is to treat the sequence of stakeholder engagement as a logistical detail: see people when their calendars allow, discuss the plan as it develops, and address concerns as they arise. In practice, the order in which stakeholders are engaged shapes the outcome as profoundly as the content of the engagement itself.

Consider two sequences for the same set of conversations. In the first, Adriana begins by speaking with the most skeptical functional head, the VP of Supply Chain who has expressed reservations about the hub model since it was first proposed. The conversation is difficult. He raises structural objections that Adriana cannot fully address because she has not yet tested the plan with the other functional heads. His concerns, unresolved and now explicitly stated, become the frame through which he will interpret everything that follows. When Adriana subsequently speaks with the other functional heads, she finds herself managing the ripple effects of that first conversation. The skeptic has mentioned his concerns informally to two of the others, and their questions now echo his framing. The steering committee meeting opens with a defensive posture that consumes the session.

In the second sequence, Adriana begins with the functional head most likely to support the plan: the VP of Commercial Operations, whose team stands to benefit most directly from the hub structure and who has a strong working relationship with the executive sponsor. This conversation produces not only an endorsement but useful input. The Commercial VP suggests a modification to the hub governance model that addresses a concern Adriana had anticipated but not yet resolved. Armed with this input and a confirmed supporter, Adriana moves to the two functional heads who are neutral but cautious. In these conversations, she can reference the Commercial VP's support, present a modified governance model that incorporates credible feedback, and explore their specific concerns from a position of growing momentum rather than initial uncertainty. By the time she reaches the skeptical Supply Chain VP, she has three conversations behind her, a refined proposal, and a coalition of support that changes the dynamic of the engagement. The skeptic's concerns are still real, but they are now being raised within a context where the balance of opinion has already shifted.

The difference between these two sequences is not a matter of manipulation. It is a matter of strategic awareness. Pre-alignment before public alignment is not political maneuvering. It is responsible leadership that prevents unnecessary conflict, ensures that proposals are tested and refined before they face collective scrutiny, and creates the conditions under which a group discussion can be productive rather than adversarial.

The Bilateral Foundation

The one-on-one conversation is the fundamental unit of multi-party negotiation. It is where interests are revealed, where proposals are tested against individual realities, where dealbreakers are identified before they surface in a group setting, and where the personal trust that sustains cooperation is built and maintained.

Bilateral conversations serve several purposes simultaneously. They are intelligence-gathering exercises: the leader learns what each stakeholder truly cares about, what their constraints are, and how they are likely to respond to specific elements of the proposal. They are testing environments: the leader can float ideas, gauge reactions, and refine the plan based on feedback that would be difficult to obtain in a formal group setting where people are conscious of being observed by peers. They are trust-building opportunities: the act of consulting someone individually, of asking for their perspective before presenting a proposal to the group, communicates respect and creates a sense of ownership in the process.

The psychological dynamic here is significant. A stakeholder who has been consulted individually before a group meeting feels that their input has been sought and, to whatever degree, incorporated. Even when the final proposal does not fully reflect their preferences, the experience of having been heard creates a predisposition toward constructive engagement rather than opposition. By contrast, a stakeholder who encounters a fully formed proposal for the first time in a group setting is more likely to feel that the decision has already been made and that their role is limited to accepting or objecting. The objection, when it comes, is often sharper and more positional than it would have been if the same concerns had been explored in a private conversation where the stakeholder felt free to think aloud.

The information gathered in bilateral conversations directly shapes what is presented to the group. Adriana's conversation with the Commercial VP produced a governance modification that strengthened the proposal. Her conversations with the two neutral functional heads revealed a shared concern about transition-period accountability that she had not anticipated and that she was able to address by adding a temporary performance protection mechanism. By the time the proposal reached the steering committee, it had been shaped by four separate conversations, each of which contributed something that improved its quality and broadened its base of support. The proposal that the group evaluated was not the same proposal that Adriana had started with, and it was better for it.

Building Coalitions Through Deliberate Sequence

Coalition building in transformation is not the formation of a political faction. It is the deliberate assembly of a base of support through a sequence of conversations designed to create momentum that carries the negotiation forward.

The logic of the sequence follows a consistent pattern. Begin with the stakeholder whose agreement is most likely and least costly. This first agreement serves a dual purpose: it validates the proposal by demonstrating that at least one credible party finds it acceptable, and it provides feedback that strengthens the proposal for subsequent conversations. Move next to stakeholders who are neutral or cautiously supportive, using the first agreement as evidence that the direction is viable and that participation is safe. With each successive conversation, the coalition grows, the proposal is refined, and the social proof accumulates. By the time the sequence reaches the most skeptical stakeholder, the context has changed. The skeptic is no longer being asked to be the first person to accept something uncertain. They are being asked whether they wish to remain outside a consensus that has already begun to form.

This sequence is not about pressuring skeptics through manufactured momentum. It is about ensuring that skeptics encounter the proposal under conditions where they can engage with it seriously rather than reflexively. A skeptic who is approached first, before any coalition exists, faces the proposal in its rawest and most vulnerable form. Their objections carry disproportionate weight because there is no counterbalancing support. A skeptic who is approached later, after the proposal has been refined by feedback from several conversations, faces a stronger and more considered version of the plan, and their objections can be assessed within a richer context.

De-escalation sequencing applies when resistance has already formed and the leader must work to loosen it rather than build support from scratch. The principle reverses the standard coalition-building order. Instead of starting with the most sympathetic party, de-escalation begins with the most reasonable skeptic: the individual whose concerns are specific, practical, and most likely to be addressable. If that skeptic's concerns can be resolved, their movement away from the resistant position weakens the coalition's cohesion. Other skeptics, observing that a respected colleague has found the engagement productive and the response adequate, recalculate their own positions. The coalition does not collapse all at once, but its solidarity weakens incrementally as individual members find that their concerns are being taken seriously and that continued opposition offers diminishing returns.

When Changes Cascade Across Functions

Multi-party negotiation in transformation is complicated further by the fact that changes in one area create dependencies and trade-offs for others. An agreement reached with one function may constrain or enable what can be offered to the next. This cascading quality requires the leader to think several conversations ahead, anticipating how the terms agreed in one negotiation will affect the terms available in subsequent ones.

Adriana's hub consolidation illustrates this dynamic. The governance modification she developed in conversation with the Commercial VP, adding a regional advisory role to the hub structure, addressed his team's concern about losing local input. But it also created a precedent. When the other functional heads learned about the advisory role, two of them immediately asked whether the same mechanism would apply to their categories. Saying yes expanded the governance structure in ways that added complexity. Saying no created an inconsistency that would need to be justified. The terms agreed in one conversation had cascaded into the next, and Adriana needed to decide before the subsequent meetings how broadly the advisory model would be applied and what conditions would govern its use.

This is the essential challenge of linked negotiations. Every agreement contains implications for agreements that have not yet been reached. A commitment to additional resources for one team during the transition creates an expectation that other teams will receive comparable support. A timeline concession for one region raises the question of whether other regions will receive the same flexibility. A side agreement that provides one stakeholder with informal assurance about a future decision creates a commitment that may conflict with what another stakeholder needs to hear.

Managing these cascading dynamics requires the leader to maintain a clear record of what has been committed, to whom, and under what conditions. It also requires the discipline to distinguish between commitments that are genuinely binding and exploratory discussions that indicated direction without constituting a promise. Side agreements and informal assurances serve a valuable function in multi-party negotiation. They provide flexibility, allow the leader to address specific concerns without formalizing every accommodation, and create the interpersonal trust that sustains cooperation. But they become dangerous when they are made inconsistently, when they contradict each other, or when they create expectations that the leader cannot honor once the full picture becomes clear. The practical discipline is to track every commitment, however informal, and to test each new commitment against those already made before offering it.

The Missteps That Harden Resistance

Sequencing errors are among the most costly mistakes in transformation negotiation because they operate in one direction. An error in content can often be corrected by revising a proposal or adjusting terms. An error in sequencing creates a dynamic that is difficult to reverse because it changes how subsequent interactions are perceived.

Engaging skeptics before supporters are mobilized is the most common and most consequential sequencing error. The skeptic's objections, raised before any supporting coalition exists, become the dominant narrative. Other stakeholders who might have been supportive hear the objections before they hear the case for the change, and their own positions form in the shadow of the skeptic's framing. Recovery requires building support after opposition has already been voiced, which is always harder than building support in advance.

Presenting finished proposals before interests have been explored produces a different kind of damage. When stakeholders encounter a fully developed plan for the first time in a formal setting, the implicit message is that their input was not needed or wanted. Even if the plan is sound, the process failure generates resentment that attaches to the content. The stakeholders' energy shifts from evaluating the proposal on its merits to asserting their right to have been consulted. Recovery requires stepping back from the formal presentation and creating the bilateral conversations that should have preceded it, which is possible but awkward and often perceived as damage control rather than genuine engagement.

Allowing early disagreements to become public before private resolution has been attempted creates a visibility trap. Once a stakeholder has stated their opposition in a group setting, walking it back becomes psychologically costly. They have committed publicly to a position, and consistency pressure, one of the influence dynamics described in Chapter 7, makes retreat feel like loss of face. A disagreement that could have been resolved in a quiet bilateral conversation becomes a fixed position that must be defended because it has been witnessed. The recovery path requires giving the stakeholder a way to adjust their position without appearing to have conceded, which often means introducing new information or a modified proposal that allows the shift to be framed as a response to changed circumstances rather than a reversal.

Making commitments to early parties that foreclose options for later ones is the cascading error described above, and its damage is proportional to the importance of the options that have been closed. Recovery requires either renegotiating the early commitment, which damages trust with the initial party, or finding creative ways to honor the commitment while still addressing the needs of later parties, which is possible but constrains the negotiation space.

Table 12.

Sequencing Planner: Template for Multi-Party Negotiation Preparation

Engagement Order	Stakeholder	Their Likely Key Interests	Goal of This Conversation	Dependencies on Prior Conversations	Risks and Constraints
1st	Most likely supporter (e.g., functional head with clearest benefit from the change).	Alignment with strategic direction; opportunity for increased influence or efficiency.	Secure endorsement; gather feedback to strengthen the proposal; identify modifications that broaden appeal.	None. This conversation sets the foundation.	Risk of over-promising in exchange for early support; commitments made here cascade into all subsequent conversations.
2nd–3rd	Neutral or cautiously supportive stakeholders.	Operational continuity; fair distribution of transition burden; adequate support during change.	Test the refined proposal; surface specific concerns; build the coalition by demonstrating that credible peers have already engaged constructively.	Depends on modifications from the 1st conversation; references to the first supporter's endorsement provide social proof.	Risk of inconsistency if the proposal evolves significantly between these conversations; need to track what has been committed.
4th–5th	Skeptical stakeholders, engaged from most reasonable to most entrenched.	Protection of team autonomy, workload, or identity; concerns about fairness; historical mistrust.	Understand the specific basis of skepticism; address concerns where possible; present the refined proposal within the context of growing coalition support.	Depends on the strength and visibility of the coalition built in prior conversations; the leader must know what can and cannot be offered given earlier commitments.	Risk of hardening resistance if the skeptic feels the coalition was built to pressure them; engagement must feel genuine, not orchestrated.
Final	Group forum (steering committee or equivalent).	Varies by participant; the group interest is in reaching a credible decision that all parties can implement.	Ratify the alignment built in bilateral conversations; address any remaining concerns publicly; secure formal commitment.	Depends on all prior conversations; the leader must know the state of every relationship and every outstanding concern before entering the room.	Risk of surprise if any stakeholder's position has shifted since the bilateral conversation; a brief check-in on the day of the meeting can prevent this.

Sequencing, coalition building, and multi-party management are ultimately a discipline of attention. The leader must hold multiple conversations in mind simultaneously, track commitments and their implications across negotiations, and anticipate how each interaction shapes the context for the next. It is demanding work, and it operates largely without recognition because successful sequencing is invisible. When it works, the steering committee meeting feels smooth and the decision appears natural. No one remarks on the six conversations that made that outcome possible. When it fails, the meeting is difficult and the failure is public. That asymmetry is characteristic of the quieter work this book describes: the effort that prevents conflict is always less visible than the effort that resolves it.

Part IV turns from the skills and dynamics of negotiation to the question of sustaining them. The remaining chapters address what happens when alignment is tested by crisis, how leaders develop the adaptive style that complex negotiation demands, how organizations can embed negotiation thinking into their processes and governance, and how the capability described throughout this book can be built, taught, and maintained over time.

PART IV

INTEGRATION AND PRACTICE

Chapter 11
Crisis Negotiation: Maintaining Alignment Under Pressure

The pilot had been running for six weeks when the system failed. The new order management platform, being tested across two distribution centers as the first phase of a supply chain transformation, experienced a data synchronization error on a Monday morning that caused approximately 1,400 customer orders to be duplicated in the processing queue. Some orders were shipped twice. Others were flagged as exceptions and held in a processing limbo that prevented them from being fulfilled at all. By Tuesday afternoon, the customer service team had received over three hundred inquiries, the operations director at the primary distribution center had reverted to the legacy system without waiting for authorization, and the story had reached the executive sponsor through two separate channels, neither of them the program team.

The program itself had been progressing well before the failure. The pilot had been carefully scoped, the technology had performed adequately in pre-launch testing, and the two distribution centers selected for the pilot were among the most capable in the network. Three regional vice presidents whose territories included downstream dependencies on the pilot sites had offered conditional support during the planning phase, expressing confidence that the pilot would demonstrate the platform's viability before any broader rollout was proposed. The executive sponsor, a senior vice president with direct board reporting responsibilities for the transformation, had cited the pilot's progress in a recent board update as evidence that the program was on track.

Within seventy-two hours of the failure, the landscape had changed completely. The three regional VPs withdrew their conditional support, each citing the failure as confirmation of concerns they had raised, with varying degrees of specificity, during the planning phase. The executive sponsor, now exposed to board-level questions about a program she had personally championed, requested an emergency review of the entire timeline. The operations director who had reverted to the legacy system became an informal symbol of practical judgment, and his decision was referenced approvingly in conversations across the organization. The program team, which had been working around the clock to diagnose and resolve the technical issue, found itself simultaneously managing a technical recovery and a collapse of stakeholder confidence that the technical fix alone could not repair.

The change leader, a program director named Carla who had managed the initiative from its inception, recognized within the first forty-eight hours that the crisis she was managing was not primarily technical. The synchronization error would be identified and corrected. The duplicate orders would be resolved. The operational damage, while real, was contained and recoverable. What was not automatically recoverable was the trust that had been built over months of careful stakeholder engagement and that had evaporated in days. The question Carla faced was not how to fix the system. It was how to rebuild alignment with stakeholders whose confidence had been shaken and whose latent concerns had been activated by the failure in ways that a technical resolution would not address.

What Crises Reveal

The most instructive aspect of a crisis in transformation is not the failure itself but what the failure's aftermath reveals about the quality of the alignment that preceded it. Agreements that were built on genuine understanding of interests and supported by ongoing engagement tend to bend under crisis pressure but not break. Stakeholders who feel that their concerns were heard and addressed, even imperfectly, are more likely to treat a setback as a problem to be solved together than as confirmation that the program was flawed from the start. Agreements built on surface consensus, where stakeholders endorsed the direction without fully committing to its implications, fracture quickly because the crisis provides a socially acceptable reason to withdraw support that was never deeply held.

The three regional VPs who withdrew their conditional support illustrate this dynamic. Their support had been genuine but shallow. They had agreed to the pilot on the basis of a reasonable business case and a credible implementation plan. What they had not done was internalize the risk of the pilot as shared risk. In their mental model, the pilot was the program team's test, and their role was to evaluate the results before deciding whether to participate further. When the failure occurred, their withdrawal was not a betrayal of a commitment. It was the exercise of a conditionality that had been present from the beginning but that the program team had not fully recognized or addressed.

Crises activate latent fears in ways that calmer periods manage to contain. The psychological dynamics are predictable: heightened loss aversion causes stakeholders to focus intensely on what they might lose rather than what might be gained; attention narrows to immediate threats rather than longer-term possibilities; behaviors revert to protective patterns, including the patterns of quiet refusal and symbolic agreement described in Chapter 2. The search for blame, which is among the most reliable features of organizational crisis response, serves a psychological function beyond assigning accountability. It restores a sense of control. If the failure can be attributed to a specific cause or a specific person, the uncertainty that the crisis introduced becomes manageable. The world makes sense again, even if the sense it makes is unflattering to the person assigned responsibility.

For the change leader, the search for blame creates a particular danger. If the leader is perceived as the source of the failure, their capacity to rebuild alignment is severely diminished. If they are perceived as the person who understands the failure and is competent to address it, their influence may actually increase. The distinction between these two perceptions is determined less by the facts of the failure than by how the leader responds in the hours and days immediately following it.

How the Landscape Shifts Under Pressure

Crises restructure the negotiation landscape by changing what stakeholders care about and who holds influence. Interests that were secondary during stable periods become primary under pressure. A regional VP who previously cared about having input into the governance design now cares only about protecting her distribution network from further disruption. A functional head who had been focused on ensuring fair resource allocation now cares about ensuring that the fallout from the failure does not land on his team. The executive sponsor, who had been concerned with strategic positioning and board-level narrative, now cares about demonstrating decisive leadership in response to a visible setback. These are not new interests. They were always present in the background. But the crisis has moved them to the foreground, displacing the interests that the program team had been engaging with during calmer conditions.

Power shifts as well, and often in directions that the existing stakeholder map does not predict. The operations director who reverted to the legacy system, a mid-level manager who would not normally feature prominently in the program's stakeholder analysis, gained significant informal authority through his decisive action during the crisis. His judgment was validated by the fact that the legacy system continued to function while the new platform was being repaired, and his status as the person who "did the right thing" gave him influence over how the failure was interpreted across the organization. The technical team responsible for diagnosing the synchronization error gained leverage because the program could not move forward without their assessment. The executive sponsor, under board pressure, became more directive and less open to the collaborative approach that had characterized her engagement during the program's earlier phases.

Carla's stakeholder map, which she had maintained carefully throughout the program, was no longer accurate. The map reflected a landscape shaped by conditions that no longer existed. The interests had shifted, the power dynamics had changed, and the coalitions that had supported the pilot were either dissolved or reconfigured around the new concern of managing the fallout. Effective crisis response required not just technical resolution but a rapid reassessment of the entire negotiation landscape.

Reassessing Alternatives and Agreement Space

The BATNA and ZOPA frameworks introduced in Chapter 6 apply in crisis conditions, but the speed at which they must be reassessed changes the nature of the exercise. In stable conditions, the leader can invest time in mapping interests, testing scenarios, and building the kind of detailed analysis that supports deliberate negotiation. In crisis, the analysis must be compressed without being abandoned. The discipline is to ask the right questions quickly rather than to answer all questions thoroughly.

The central question in crisis reassessment is not "How do we get back on track?" This question assumes that the pre-crisis plan remains the correct destination and that the crisis is merely a detour. It may be, but it may not. The more useful question is "What does each stakeholder need right now?" This question accepts that the landscape has changed and focuses on the current reality rather than the previous plan.

For Carla, the answers to this question were specific and actionable. The executive sponsor needed a credible narrative for the board: not a minimization of the failure, but a clear account of what happened, what was being done about it, and what the implications were for the program's timeline and scope. The regional VPs needed assurance that no broader rollout would be proposed until the failure had been fully understood and addressed, and that their conditional support was genuinely conditional rather than a formality that the program team intended to override. The operations director needed acknowledgment that his decision to revert had been correct, which was both factually accurate and strategically important because dismissing his judgment would have alienated a person who had become an influential voice in how the failure was interpreted. The program team needed protection from being scapegoated and a clear mandate to focus on diagnosis and resolution rather than on managing political fallout.

Each of these needs defined a different negotiation with different terms. The ZOPA for each had shifted. The sponsor's zone of acceptable outcomes now required visible program adjustments, not just a technical fix. The regional VPs' zone had narrowed to the point where only a genuine pause in expansion planning would satisfy their conditions. The operations director's zone was defined by respect and recognition rather than by any specific programmatic outcome. Mapping these revised zones, even quickly and imperfectly, gave Carla a working picture of what agreements were possible in the new landscape and where the gaps remained.

Rebuilding Trust Through Competence and Honesty

The temptation in crisis is to manage the narrative. To frame the failure as an isolated incident, to emphasize the lessons learned, to pivot quickly to a revised plan that demonstrates confidence and forward momentum. This approach is understandable, and in some organizational cultures it is expected. It is also, in most cases, counterproductive.

Stakeholders who have just watched a significant failure unfold are alert to exactly this kind of response. They have seen programs minimize setbacks before. They have heard the language of "lessons learned" deployed as a shield against accountability. When the change leader's first response to a crisis is to reframe it, the stakeholders hear not reassurance but evasion, and their trust erodes further rather than beginning to recover.

The more effective approach begins with acknowledgment. Not performative contrition, not excessive self-blame, but a clear and specific statement of what happened and what its implications are. Carla's initial communication to the steering committee was direct: the synchronization error had caused measurable operational disruption, the root cause had been identified, and the technical resolution was underway. She did not minimize the impact or offer premature reassurance about the timeline. She stated what she knew, acknowledged what she did not yet know, and committed to providing a full assessment within a defined timeframe.

This kind of honesty accomplishes several things simultaneously. It demonstrates competence, because a leader who can describe a problem clearly is perceived as more capable of solving it than a leader who appears to be avoiding the description. It establishes credibility, because stakeholders trust a person who acknowledges difficulty more than a person who insists that everything is under control when it visibly is not. And it creates the conditions for a new agreement by defining the current reality from which that agreement must be built.

The new agreement itself must be modest enough to be credible. In Carla's case, the post-crisis agreement involved four elements: a defined pause in any expansion planning until the technical assessment was complete, an independent review of the pilot's design to determine whether the failure reflected a systemic issue or an isolated error, a commitment to share the review's findings transparently with all stakeholders, and a revised decision point at which the steering committee would evaluate whether to proceed, modify, or terminate the program based on the review's conclusions. None of these elements represented what Carla would have chosen under ideal conditions. Collectively, they represented what was achievable given the current state of stakeholder trust, and they preserved the possibility of forward movement once that trust began to recover.

In crisis, trust is rebuilt through demonstrated competence and sustained honesty, not through communication strategy. Every interaction in the weeks following a crisis is evaluated by stakeholders through a heightened filter. Promises kept, even small ones, accumulate credibility. Promises broken, even inadvertently, confirm the narrative of unreliability. The leader who survives a crisis with their influence intact is the one who consistently does what they said they would do, provides information when they said they would provide it, and treats each stakeholder's concerns with the same seriousness they would want their own concerns to receive.

What the Crisis Taught

Every crisis in transformation reveals information that was previously hidden, and the leader who treats the aftermath only as a recovery exercise misses the most valuable opportunity the crisis provides. The failure of Carla's pilot exposed several features of the stakeholder landscape that her pre-crisis mapping had not captured. The regional VPs' support had been thinner than it appeared, conditional in ways that the program team had not fully tested. The operations director's informal influence was far greater than his formal role suggested. The executive sponsor's engagement style shifted under pressure from collaborative to directive, which was useful information for future negotiations. The program team's credibility was more fragile than Carla had assumed, dependent on an unbroken record of competent execution that the crisis had interrupted.

Each of these revelations represented an opportunity to strengthen the alignment for the next phase of the program. The regional VPs' conditionality, now explicit rather than implicit, could be addressed directly through genuine shared risk structures rather than assumed through optimistic interpretation. The operations director could be engaged as a stakeholder whose influence warranted direct relationship management rather than being treated as a mid-level implementer. The sponsor's directive tendency under pressure could be anticipated and managed through earlier and more frequent communication during periods of uncertainty.

The temptation after a crisis is to restore the status quo ante, to get back to where things were before the failure occurred. The more productive response is to use the post-crisis clarity to build something stronger than what existed before. The agreements that follow a crisis, if they are built on honest acknowledgment of what the crisis revealed, tend to be more durable than the agreements they replace. They are built on tested understanding rather than untested assumptions, and they carry the weight of shared experience rather than shared optimism. The program that survives a crisis and emerges with stronger alignment has achieved something that no amount of careful planning could have produced on its own: proof, visible to all parties, that the collaboration can withstand pressure and that the commitments made to each other are real.

The remaining chapters turn from navigating specific situations to building sustained capability. Chapter 12 examines how leaders develop the adaptive style that allows them to move between empathy and assertiveness as different conversations demand. Chapter 13 addresses how negotiation thinking can be embedded in organizational processes rather than remaining dependent on individual skill. And the final chapter explores how the capability described throughout this book can be taught, scaled, and sustained across the teams and institutions that carry transformation forward.

Chapter 12
Developing an Adaptive Negotiation Style

The change leader had built her reputation on the quality of her relationships. Over fifteen years in transformation work, she had developed a natural ability to make people feel heard, to create safe spaces for difficult conversations, and to draw out the interests beneath stated positions through patience and genuine curiosity. These qualities had served her exceptionally well during the first phase of a global process standardization initiative. Stakeholders who were cautious about the program opened up to her in one-on-one conversations. Teams that had resisted earlier programs found her approach refreshing. The early months of the initiative produced a level of stakeholder engagement that the executive sponsor described as the strongest she had seen in any comparable program.

The problem became visible during a steering committee meeting in the seventh month. The regional head for Central Europe, a direct and experienced operator who had been testing the boundaries of the program's timeline for several weeks, stated flatly that his region would not meet the agreed implementation date and that he expected the program to accommodate a six-month delay. His tone was not hostile but it was firm, and it carried the implicit message that he had made his decision and was informing the committee rather than requesting permission. The change leader's instinct, refined over years of relationship-centered practice, was to acknowledge his concerns, explore the underlying pressures, and find a collaborative path forward. She began to do exactly that, asking what specific constraints were driving the request and whether additional support might change the picture.

The regional head interpreted her response as an opening. He expanded his position, adding conditions that had not been mentioned before: a dedicated implementation team for his region, a modified governance structure that would give him greater control over the local rollout, and a commitment that no other region's timeline would be adjusted to compensate for his delay. By the end of the conversation, what had begun as a timeline concern had become a comprehensive renegotiation of the program's terms for Central Europe, conducted in a public forum where every other regional head was watching and calculating what similar assertiveness might yield for their own position.

The change leader recognized, as she reflected on the meeting afterward, that her strengths had become vulnerabilities. The empathetic, exploratory approach that built trust in bilateral conversations had been exploited in a group setting by a stakeholder who was not seeking understanding but testing limits. Her instinct to accommodate had signaled flexibility where the program needed firmness. Other regional heads who had been prepared to meet the original timeline were now reconsidering, not because their circumstances had changed but because the meeting had demonstrated that the timeline was negotiable for anyone willing to push hard enough. The credibility of the program's commitments, which had been carefully built over months, had been weakened in a single conversation by a style of engagement that was excellent in one context and inadequate in another.

No single negotiation style is sufficient for the range of situations that transformation leaders encounter. The capacity to move between empathy, assertiveness, and analytical rigor depending on what each conversation requires is not a fixed trait. It is a skill that develops through deliberate practice and honest self-assessment.

Understanding Your Defaults

Most leaders negotiate from a default orientation that they have developed over time through a combination of temperament, professional training, and the accumulated lessons of experience. Some lead naturally with empathy. They are attuned to emotional undercurrents, skilled at building trust, and instinctively oriented toward understanding before advocating. Others lead with analysis. They are most comfortable when the conversation is grounded in data, logic, and structured evaluation of options, and they tend to respond to emotional dynamics by redirecting the discussion toward facts. Still others lead with assertiveness. They are direct, clear about their own position, and comfortable with the tension that arises when interests conflict openly.

None of these orientations is inherently superior to the others, and each produces excellent results in the situations it is suited for. Empathetic leaders excel in conversations where the stakeholder's resistance stems from fear, identity threat, or unacknowledged concerns. Analytical leaders excel when the dispute is genuinely about data interpretation, risk assessment, or the evaluation of trade-offs. Assertive leaders excel when boundaries must be maintained, when ambiguity needs to be resolved through clarity rather than further exploration, and when the cost of accommodation would be borne by parties who are not present in the conversation.

The problem arises not from the default itself but from its automatic application to situations that require something different. The empathetic leader who responds to every form of resistance with exploration and accommodation will eventually encounter a stakeholder who interprets that approach as weakness. The analytical leader who meets every emotional objection with data will eventually face a conversation where the stakeholder feels unheard regardless of how compelling the analysis is. The assertive leader who responds to every disagreement with clarity and directness will eventually damage a relationship that required patience and careful listening before it could support honest engagement.

The first step toward adaptive style is self-awareness about these patterns. Not self-criticism, which tends to produce either defensiveness or overcorrection, but honest observation of how you naturally respond under different kinds of pressure. Several questions can guide this observation. How do you respond when a stakeholder raises an emotional objection to something you believe is well-supported by evidence? Do you lean toward acknowledging the emotion, addressing the evidence, or reaffirming the decision? When do you feel most uncomfortable in a negotiation? Is it when the other person is visibly upset, when the conversation becomes contentious, when the data is ambiguous, or when you are being asked to make a commitment you are not certain you can keep? What kind of resistance triggers you to either accommodate or escalate? Is it personal criticism, procedural obstruction, passive withdrawal, or aggressive confrontation? The answers to these questions are not measures of competence. They are data about the conditions under which your default style is most likely to be activated, and awareness of those conditions is the foundation on which adaptability is built.

Matching the Approach to the Situation

The framework for choosing which approach to lead with in a given conversation connects directly to the concepts developed throughout this book. Each of the major dynamics described in earlier chapters suggests a different primary register.

When the stakeholder's resistance stems from identity threat, fear of exposure, or concerns that have not been acknowledged, empathy should lead. The material in Chapters 4 and 8 describes the psychological mechanisms at work in these situations: unspoken fears shaping stated demands, identity-based interests that cannot be addressed through operational adjustments alone, and emotional responses that carry information about what the stakeholder values. In these conversations, the leader's primary task is to create conditions where the real concern can surface. This requires patience, genuine curiosity, and the willingness to let the conversation unfold at a pace the stakeholder controls rather than a pace the program requires. Assertiveness in these moments, however well-intentioned, closes the door that the conversation needs to open.

When boundaries must be maintained, when a stakeholder is testing limits, or when the cost of accommodation would fall on parties who are not in the room, assertiveness should lead. The change leader in the opening scene faced exactly this situation. The regional head was not expressing a hidden fear or an unacknowledged concern. He was probing the program's resolve, and the appropriate response was to hold the line clearly and specifically. Assertiveness in this register does not mean aggression or rigidity. It means stating what is and is not negotiable, explaining why, and doing so with enough confidence that the stakeholder understands the boundary is real. The most effective assertive statements combine clarity about the limit with respect for the person encountering it: "The implementation date is a commitment we have made to all regions, and adjusting it for one region would undermine the credibility of the commitment to every other. I want to find ways to support your team within that timeline, and I am genuinely open to discussing what that support looks like. But the date itself is not something I can reopen."

When the dispute is genuinely about competing interpretations of data, differing assessments of risk, or the evaluation of trade-offs between concrete options, analysis should lead. Chapter 6's treatment of BATNA, ZOPA, and leverage describes situations where the most productive conversation is one grounded in structured evaluation of alternatives. In these moments, emotional attunement and assertive boundary-setting are less useful than the ability to lay out the options clearly, assess their implications rigorously, and guide the conversation toward the option that best addresses the full range of interests at stake.

Most conversations require a blend rather than a pure application of any single approach. The question is not which register to use exclusively but which to lead with, and the answer depends on an accurate reading of what the conversation actually requires at each stage.

Reading the Room in Real Time

The concepts described in the preceding section are useful in preparation, when the leader has time to assess the situation and plan an approach. The greater challenge is reading what is happening during a conversation and adjusting accordingly. Stakeholders do not announce that their resistance stems from identity threat rather than operational concern. They do not signal in advance whether they are testing limits or expressing genuine fear. The leader must interpret these dynamics in real time, based on signals that are often ambiguous and that require judgment rather than formula.

Tone shifts are among the most reliable indicators. A stakeholder whose voice becomes quieter or more careful is often approaching a subject that carries emotional weight. A stakeholder whose tone becomes sharper or more clipped is often moving from genuine inquiry to positional defense. The difference matters because each calls for a different response: the quieter tone invites the leader to slow down and create space, while the sharper tone signals that the leader should hold steady rather than yielding ground.

The distinction between genuine questions and rhetorical challenges is equally important and frequently misread. A genuine question seeks information: "How will the transition affect our team's workload during the first quarter?" A rhetorical challenge uses the form of a question to assert a position: "How can we possibly be expected to maintain service levels during a transition of this scale?" The first invites a substantive answer. The second invites acknowledgment of the concern behind it. Responding to a rhetorical challenge with data addresses a question that was not actually being asked and often produces frustration rather than clarity.

Silence is the most ambiguous signal and the one that leaders most frequently mishandle. When a stakeholder falls silent after a statement or proposal, the silence may indicate thoughtful processing, in which case the leader should wait. It may indicate confusion, in which case clarification is needed. Or it may indicate withdrawal, a quiet disengagement that signals the conversation has moved past the stakeholder's comfort zone or has failed to address what they actually care about. Distinguishing among these requires attention to context: what preceded the silence, whether the stakeholder was actively engaged before it occurred, and what their body language communicates. The most common error is to fill the silence prematurely with more information or a revised offer, when the most productive response would have been to wait and let the stakeholder reengage on their own terms.

Adjusting Without Losing Credibility

Recognizing that the current approach is not working is only useful if the leader can shift to a different one without appearing inconsistent or manipulative. The mechanics of mid-conversation adjustment are simpler than they may appear, but they require a degree of transparency that many leaders find uncomfortable.

The most effective technique is naming what you are doing. "I realize I have been focused on the data, and I think there is something more important going on here. Can you help me understand what is really concerning you about this?" This kind of statement accomplishes several things at once: it acknowledges that the current approach is insufficient, it signals genuine interest in the stakeholder's experience, and it creates a transition point in the conversation that both parties can recognize. The transparency itself builds trust, because it demonstrates that the leader is paying attention to the conversation's quality rather than simply executing a script.

Questions serve as natural transition mechanisms. A leader who has been operating in an assertive register and senses that the stakeholder has withdrawn can shift by asking an open question that invites the stakeholder back into the conversation: "I have been very clear about what the program needs. What I have not done well enough is ask what you need. What would make this work for your team?" The question changes the dynamic without requiring the leader to retract anything they have said. It opens a new register alongside the existing one rather than replacing it.

Knowing when to pause a conversation rather than forcing it to conclusion is perhaps the most undervalued skill in negotiation. There are moments when the most productive response to a stalled or deteriorating conversation is to stop it. "I think we have reached a point where we both need some time to think about this. Can we come back to it Thursday?" A pause is not a failure. It is a recognition that not every negotiation reaches resolution in a single sitting, and that allowing both parties time to process can produce better outcomes than pushing through when the conversation has lost its productive quality. The decision to pause requires confidence, because the instinct in most organizational cultures is to finish what you started. But a conversation concluded under pressure often produces agreements that are less durable than agreements reached after reflection.

Expanding Your Range

Adaptive style is not a technique that can be learned from a chapter in a book. It is a capacity that develops over time through deliberate practice, honest reflection, and the willingness to operate outside your comfort zone in controlled ways.

The most practical form of deliberate practice involves choosing, before a specific conversation, to lead with an approach that is not your default. The empathetic leader who knows she needs to hold a boundary in an upcoming meeting prepares by formulating the specific language she will use to state the limit, rehearsing it until it feels natural rather than forced, and identifying the moment in the conversation where the boundary is most likely to be tested. The assertive leader who knows he needs to create space for a stakeholder's emotional concerns prepares by committing to listen for at least three minutes before responding, and by preparing open-ended questions that invite the stakeholder to describe their experience rather than defend their position. The practice is not about suppressing the default. It is about expanding the repertoire so that the default becomes one option among several rather than the only available response.

Debriefing conversations after they occur builds the observational habit that adaptive style requires. The questions are straightforward: What was the other person actually responding to? Was there a moment where the conversation shifted, and what caused it? Was there a point where a different approach would have produced a better outcome? These are not questions of self-judgment. They are questions of craft, asked with the same curiosity that a musician brings to reviewing a performance or an athlete brings to studying game film. The goal is pattern recognition: understanding which approaches produce which results in which contexts, so that the next conversation can be entered with greater situational awareness.

Feedback from trusted colleagues, particularly those who have observed the leader in negotiation, provides information that self-observation cannot. Most people have blind spots about their own negotiation style, tendencies that are visible to others but invisible to themselves. A colleague who says "You tend to soften your position when the other person shows frustration" or "You become more analytical when the conversation gets emotional" is offering data that the leader can use to calibrate their approach. Seeking this feedback requires vulnerability, which is why it should be sought from people whose judgment is trusted and whose intent is supportive rather than evaluative.

The long-term goal is fluency: the ability to move between empathy, analytical rigor, and assertive clarity with the same naturalness that a skilled conversationalist moves between topics. This fluency does not mean abandoning authenticity. It means recognizing that authenticity is not a single fixed style but the honest expression of a leader's full range of capabilities, deployed in service of conversations that matter. The leader who can hold a boundary without damaging a relationship, who can acknowledge emotion without losing analytical clarity, and who can shift approach mid-conversation without appearing manipulative, has developed a capacity that makes every other skill in this book more effective.

The skills and principles developed throughout this book can be embedded in organizational processes and governance structures, so that effective negotiation becomes a feature of how the organization operates rather than a quality that depends on the presence of a single skilled individual. What that embedding looks like in practice requires a shift in perspective: from the individual conversation to the institutional design.

Chapter 13
Designing Negotiation-Driven Processes

For three consecutive quarters, the same argument repeated itself in the same conference room. The transformation program at a North American financial services company had established a quarterly resource allocation review as part of its governance framework. The review was designed to adjust staffing and budget across the program's five workstreams based on evolving priorities and progress. In principle, it was a sensible mechanism: a regular opportunity to rebalance resources as the program learned more about what each workstream required. In practice, it had become a quarterly zero-sum competition that consumed weeks of preparation, produced hours of contentious debate, and left at least two of the five workstream leads feeling that the outcome was unfair.

The pattern was remarkably consistent. In the weeks before each review, workstream leads would build cases for why their allocation should be maintained or increased. Each case was framed in terms of risk: what would go wrong if resources were reduced, what milestones would slip, what dependencies would be affected. The review itself functioned as a negotiation in which each lead advocated for their own workstream while the program director attempted to balance competing claims against a fixed resource pool. The leads who argued most effectively, or whose workstreams had the most visible executive attention, tended to receive favorable outcomes. Those who were less forceful, or whose work was less immediately visible, absorbed the reductions. After each review, the leads who felt disadvantaged carried that perception into the next quarter, which intensified their advocacy and deepened the adversarial dynamic.

The program director, a thoughtful leader named Marcus who had managed large initiatives before, spent the first two cycles trying to manage the conflict through better facilitation. He prepared more detailed analyses, created more transparent scoring criteria, and invested time in bilateral conversations before each review to understand each lead's concerns. These efforts improved the quality of the conversation marginally but did not change its fundamental character. The third cycle was when he recognized that the problem was not the people in the room or the quality of the facilitation. The problem was the process itself. The governance structure had been designed in a way that made adversarial behavior rational. Each quarter, five leads competed for a fixed pool, and the outcome depended on their relative advocacy skills rather than on any structural mechanism for determining what a fair and effective allocation would look like. No amount of negotiation skill, including his own, would change the dynamic as long as the process continued to produce it.

The most durable application of negotiation thinking is not the conduct of individual conversations but the design of processes that make good outcomes structural. When fairness, transparency, and interest-alignment are built into how decisions are made, the organization becomes less dependent on the presence of a skilled negotiator in every room. Negotiation principles shift from personal capabilities exercised in specific moments to organizational capabilities embedded in how the institution operates.

Incentive Design: Making Cooperation Rational

Chapter 9 introduced the game-theoretic principle that behavior is shaped by incentive structures and that changing outcomes requires changing the structure rather than persuading individuals. That principle applies with particular force to the design of organizational processes during transformation. When the incentive landscape rewards behaviors that conflict with the transformation's objectives, the best negotiated agreements will erode as soon as the conversation ends and the structural incentives reassert themselves.

The most persistent misalignment in transformation involves individual metrics pulling against collective goals. During transformation, the behaviors that matter most are often collaborative: sharing resources across workstreams, absorbing short-term cost to enable a collective benefit, investing time in coordination that does not appear on any individual scorecard. Yet most organizations measure and reward individual performance. A workstream lead who diverts resources to support a struggling peer workstream may improve the program's overall trajectory but will see her own metrics suffer. A functional head who accepts a delayed timeline to accommodate a cross-functional dependency makes the right collective decision but reports a less impressive result to his own leadership. As long as these structural contradictions persist, cooperation requires altruism, and altruism is not a reliable basis for organizational behavior.

Shared metrics are the most direct tool for resolving this contradiction. When two or more groups are measured against a common outcome that requires collaboration to achieve, the incentive to cooperate becomes individually rational rather than individually costly. Marcus's resource allocation process could have incorporated a shared metric tied to overall program milestone achievement rather than individual workstream performance, which would have shifted each lead's calculus from "How do I maximize my allocation?" to "How do we allocate in a way that maximizes the collective result?" The metric must carry real weight. A shared metric that is tracked but not tied to performance evaluation, recognition, or resource decisions will be treated as symbolic, and the individual metrics will continue to drive behavior.

Joint accountability operates on the same principle at the level of decision ownership. When a milestone or outcome is the shared accountability of multiple parties, each party has a rational interest in the success of the others, which creates a structural basis for mutual support rather than mutual indifference. The accountability must be genuinely shared, meaning that all parties bear visible consequences for failure and share visible credit for success. A nominal shared accountability where one party absorbs the consequences while others are effectively insulated will be recognized for what it is and will not change behavior.

Recognition that values collective contribution addresses the cultural dimension of incentive design. In most organizations, the stories that are told about success, the examples that are celebrated in leadership communications, and the behaviors that are rewarded in promotion decisions emphasize individual achievement. During transformation, deliberately recognizing and celebrating collaborative contributions, the leader who modified her plan to accommodate a dependency, the team that shared capacity with a peer group during a peak period, the function that absorbed short-term cost to enable a long-term collective benefit, signals that the organization values cooperation as a form of excellence rather than treating it as a charitable act. This signal, reinforced consistently over time, shifts the social incentive alongside the structural one.

Mechanism Design: Building Fairness Into the Structure

Incentive design addresses what people are motivated to do. Mechanism design addresses how decisions are made, structuring the process so that fair and effective outcomes emerge from the procedure itself rather than depending on the skill or goodwill of the participants.

Marcus's resource allocation process failed because its mechanism was essentially unstructured advocacy: each lead argued for their share, and the outcome reflected the balance of persuasive force in the room. A better mechanism would have reduced the role of advocacy and increased the role of structured criteria. Transparent allocation principles, agreed in advance and applied consistently, reduce the perception of unfairness and diminish the adversarial dynamic that unstructured competition produces. If every participant knows that allocations are determined by a defined set of factors, weighted according to agreed priorities, the quarterly review becomes a calibration exercise rather than a contest. Disagreements can still occur, but they occur about the criteria and their application rather than about the raw distribution of resources.

Rotating decision rights provide another structural mechanism for embedding fairness. When certain decisions must be made that affect multiple parties unequally, rotating the authority to make those decisions ensures that no single party consistently bears the burden or enjoys the advantage of control. The rotation must be genuine, not symbolic, and the decision rights must carry real consequence. This approach is particularly effective for recurring operational decisions that would otherwise require constant renegotiation: which region absorbs overflow work during peak periods, which function provides surge capacity when a program accelerates, or which team takes the lead on cross-functional coordination for a given quarter.

Pre-agreed escalation paths with clear triggers address the inevitable moments when process-level decisions cannot resolve a disagreement. The value of pre-agreement is that it removes the ambiguity and political calculation from the act of escalating. When the triggers are defined in advance, such as a resource gap exceeding a certain threshold, a timeline delay beyond a specified number of days, or a stakeholder formally invoking the escalation mechanism, the escalation is experienced as part of the process rather than as a political act. This reduces the reluctance that many leaders feel about escalating, a reluctance that often causes issues to fester until they have grown far more difficult to resolve than they would have been if addressed earlier.

Structured processes for raising and resolving concerns create a legitimate channel for the kinds of issues that might otherwise surface as resistance. When there is no formal mechanism for expressing a concern about workload distribution, timeline feasibility, or perceived unfairness, those concerns find informal channels: hallway conversations, coalition formation, quiet refusal. A structured process that invites concerns, routes them to the appropriate decision-maker, and provides a visible response does not eliminate disagreement, but it ensures that disagreement is addressed within the governance framework rather than outside it.

Feedback Loops: Detecting What the Process Cannot See

Processes, however well designed, operate on assumptions about conditions that change over time. An incentive structure that aligned with the program's needs in its first phase may become counterproductive in its second. A governance mechanism that worked when five stakeholder groups were involved may need adjustment when the program expands to include eight. The process itself cannot detect these shifts. That function belongs to feedback loops: systematic channels through which the organization learns whether its processes are producing the intended effects and whether alignment is holding or weakening.

Formal feedback channels include structured check-ins with key stakeholders at defined intervals, sentiment assessments that capture how the program is being experienced across different groups, and milestone reviews that evaluate not only whether targets were met but how the process of meeting them affected stakeholder relationships and commitment. Each of these instruments provides a different kind of information. Check-ins capture individual perspectives. Sentiment assessments reveal patterns across groups. Milestone reviews connect process outcomes to relationship outcomes, which is the level at which most process failures become visible.

Informal channels are equally important and often more revealing. Designated listening posts, individuals embedded in different parts of the organization who are trusted by the program team and by their local colleagues, can detect shifts in sentiment and emerging concerns long before they appear in formal reporting. Walking-the-floor practices, where program leaders spend time in the operational environments affected by the transformation rather than managing exclusively through governance forums, provide unfiltered exposure to how the change is actually being experienced. Trusted intermediaries, people who maintain relationships across organizational boundaries and who are willing to share what they are hearing, provide early warning of coalition shifts, emerging resistance, and concerns that stakeholders have not yet raised through official channels.

The critical principle governing all feedback loops, formal and informal alike, is that feedback must be acted upon visibly. A check-in that surfaces a legitimate concern, followed by no visible response, teaches the stakeholder that the check-in is performative. A sentiment assessment that reveals declining confidence in the program's fairness, followed by no adjustment, teaches the organization that the assessment is a ritual rather than a genuine instrument of governance. Each instance of unacted-upon feedback erodes the credibility of the channel, and once a channel loses credibility, it ceases to produce honest information. The commitment to feedback loops is therefore a commitment to response, which means that the organization must have the capacity and the willingness to adjust its processes based on what the loops reveal. Feedback without response is worse than no feedback at all, because it creates the appearance of listening while confirming the suspicion that no one is actually paying attention.

Embedding Negotiation in Governance

The final dimension of process design involves integrating negotiation thinking into the governance structures through which the transformation is managed. Most governance forums, steering committees, program reviews, working groups, and escalation meetings are designed to make decisions and track progress. They are not typically designed to surface interests, test alignment, or detect the early signals of misalignment that this book has argued are essential to sustaining cooperation. The result is governance that functions well for its stated purpose but that misses the human dynamics operating beneath the formal agenda.

The adjustment does not require creating parallel structures or adding new forums to an already crowded governance calendar. It requires embedding specific practices into the forums that already exist. A steering committee that allocates the first fifteen minutes of each session to an open discussion of emerging concerns before moving to decision items creates space for interests to surface. The practice must be genuine: if the fifteen minutes are consistently compressed to accommodate a crowded agenda, the signal is that concerns are less important than decisions, and stakeholders will stop raising them. A program review that includes a brief assessment of stakeholder sentiment alongside progress metrics integrates alignment monitoring into the existing reporting cadence. The assessment does not need to be elaborate. A simple structured question, "Where has alignment strengthened since the last review, and where has it weakened?" asked of the program team and answered with specificity, provides information that traditional progress metrics cannot.

Escalation processes benefit particularly from the integration of negotiation thinking. In most governance frameworks, escalation is triggered by a disagreement that cannot be resolved at the current level and is elevated to a higher authority for decision. This structure is necessary, but it often produces outcomes that address the surface disagreement while leaving the underlying interests unresolved, because the escalation process is designed to produce a ruling rather than an agreement. Requiring that escalation submissions include an interest map, a brief description of the interests at stake for each party, alongside the factual summary of the disagreement, changes the nature of the escalation. The decision-maker receives not only the competing positions but the information needed to design a resolution that addresses what each party actually needs. This does not guarantee a better outcome, but it creates the conditions under which a better outcome becomes more likely.

Table 13.

Process Design Checklist: Embedding Negotiation in Governance Forums

Governance Forum	Negotiation Elements to Embed	Information to Gather Beforehand	Outputs to Produce
Steering Committee	Open discussion of emerging concerns before decision items; explicit check on stakeholder sentiment; review of any commitments made in bilateral conversations that affect the group.	Updated stakeholder map noting any shifts since the last session; summary of concerns raised through formal and informal channels; status of any commitments from prior sessions.	Decisions that reflect explored interests, not only presented positions; documented commitments with clear ownership; identified follow-up conversations needed before the next session.
Program Review	Stakeholder alignment assessment alongside progress metrics; review of incentive and metric alignment; identification of emerging friction patterns.	Progress data, stakeholder sentiment data, and any feedback from formal or informal channels; assessment of whether current incentives are supporting or undermining collaboration.	Adjusted priorities informed by both operational progress and stakeholder dynamics; flagged areas where process adjustments may be needed; updated risk assessment that includes alignment risks.
Working Group	Structured interest exploration before problem-solving; rotating facilitation to ensure multiple perspectives are heard; explicit documentation of trade-offs considered and rejected.	Each participant's key concerns and constraints; any relevant commitments or agreements from higher governance levels that constrain the working group's options.	Recommendations that reflect multiple interests rather than the dominant voice in the room; transparent record of trade-offs for use in subsequent governance discussions.
Escalation Forum	Requirement for interest mapping alongside factual summary of disagreement; exploration of alternative resolutions before a ruling is issued; commitment to communicate the rationale for the decision to all affected parties.	Interest maps from the escalating parties; summary of resolution attempts to date; assessment of the implications of each possible outcome for the broader program.	A resolution that addresses underlying interests where possible; clear rationale communicated to all parties; follow-up plan to monitor whether the resolution is holding.

The process designs described in this chapter do not replace the negotiation skills developed in earlier chapters. They create the conditions under which those skills can operate more effectively and, crucially, in which good outcomes can occur even when the most skilled negotiator is not in the room. When fairness is structural rather than dependent on individual judgment, when incentives reward cooperation rather than requiring it as an act of goodwill, when feedback channels are credible and responsive, and when governance forums are designed to surface interests alongside decisions, the organization becomes more capable of sustaining alignment across the full arc of a transformation. The final chapter turns to the question of how all of this, the skills, the processes, and the underlying discipline of negotiation, can be taught, scaled, and sustained beyond any single program or any single leader.

Chapter 14
Building the Capability: Teaching, Scaling, and Sustaining

Two years into a multi-phase operational transformation at a healthcare services company, the senior program leader was asked by the incoming chief operating officer to explain what had changed between the first year and the second. The numbers told part of the story. Milestone achievement rates had improved. Stakeholder escalations had decreased. The average time to resolve cross-functional disagreements had dropped from several weeks to days. But the numbers did not capture the shift that the program leader considered most significant.

In the first year, the transformation's progress had depended heavily on three people: the program leader herself, a deputy with strong facilitation skills, and an external advisor who had deep experience in organizational negotiation. These three individuals conducted nearly all of the critical stakeholder conversations, prepared for every steering committee meeting, and managed the bilateral engagements that kept the program's coalition intact. When any of the three was unavailable, the quality of the engagement dropped noticeably. Conversations became more positional. Concerns that would have been surfaced in a skilled one-on-one went undetected until they appeared as resistance in formal governance forums. The program advanced, but its human infrastructure was fragile, concentrated in too few individuals and too dependent on their continued presence and attention.

In the second year, the program leader made a deliberate decision to invest in building negotiation capability across the program's broader leadership team. Over a period of four months, thirty change leads received structured training in interest mapping, stakeholder engagement, BATNA analysis, and framing. They practiced through simulations designed around the program's actual dynamics. They received coaching before critical conversations and debriefed those conversations afterward. They were given tools, not as additional process obligations but as preparation aids that reduced the cognitive burden of applying what they had learned.

The effect was not immediate, but it was cumulative and, by the end of the second year, unmistakable. Resistance was being detected earlier because thirty people were now paying attention to the behavioral signals described in this book, not just three. Agreements were more durable because the conversations that produced them were conducted with greater skill and greater attention to the interests beneath stated positions. The program accelerated not because the strategy had changed or because the executive sponsor had applied more pressure, but because the organization's capacity to sustain alignment across dozens of simultaneous conversations had expanded by an order of magnitude. The program leader's reflection to the COO was simple: "We stopped relying on a few skilled negotiators and started building the skill into the team. That changed everything."

The preceding chapters developed a set of concepts, frameworks, and practices for the individual leader. The transition from individual skill to organizational capability is what this chapter addresses: how those same ideas can be taught, practiced, embedded in organizational routines, and sustained over time so that the capability outlasts any single program or any single person who helped build it.

Designing Workshops That Teach Through Practice

The most common failure in organizational training is the assumption that understanding a concept is the same as being able to apply it. A change lead who can explain the distinction between positions and interests in a classroom setting may still default to positional negotiation in a real stakeholder conversation, because the cognitive demands of a live interaction are qualitatively different from the demands of an educational exercise. Effective workshop design bridges this gap by grounding the learning in practice from the beginning rather than building toward practice from a foundation of theory.

The design principle that produces the strongest results is to use the participants' real situations as the primary material. Rather than constructing generic case studies about fictional organizations, workshops that draw on the program's actual stakeholder dynamics, its real conflicts, its genuine points of friction, create learning that transfers directly to the work the participants will return to. A workshop exercise in which a change lead builds an Interest Map for a stakeholder she will meet the following week produces deeper learning and more immediate value than the same exercise applied to a hypothetical scenario. The emotional engagement is higher because the stakes are real, and the feedback from peers and facilitators is more useful because it addresses a situation the participant genuinely needs to navigate.

The workshop structure that works best follows a cycle of brief conceptual introduction followed by extended practice followed by structured debriefing. The conceptual introduction should be concise, no more than fifteen to twenty minutes for each framework, and should focus on what the framework does rather than on its theoretical origins. The practice should consume the majority of the workshop time, with participants working through exercises that require them to apply the framework to their own situations. The debriefing is where the deepest learning occurs, because it is where participants articulate what they discovered, where they struggled, and how the framework changed their interpretation of the situation. Without the debrief, the practice remains experience without reflection, and the learning it contains may not be extracted.

The frameworks that translate most effectively into workshop formats are Interest Maps (Chapter 5), BATNA analysis (Chapter 6), framing exercises (Chapter 7), and the sequencing planner (Chapter 10). Each of these is structured enough to provide scaffolding for the exercise but open enough to accommodate the specific dynamics of the participant's situation. Stakeholder ecosystem mapping (Chapter 3) is better suited to a team exercise than an individual one, because the value of the map increases when multiple perspectives contribute to it. Behavioral bias recognition (Chapter 8) works well as a pattern-identification exercise where participants review actual program dynamics and identify which biases may be operating, which builds the observational habit that Chapter 8 argues is essential.

Simulations That Replicate Real Dynamics

Workshops develop individual competence with specific tools. Simulations develop the ability to apply those tools under conditions that approximate the complexity, ambiguity, and interpersonal pressure of real transformation negotiations.

An effective simulation replicates the features that make real negotiations difficult. Participants are assigned roles with genuine interest conflicts, not theatrical opposition but the kind of legitimate, overlapping, partially compatible interests that characterize actual stakeholder dynamics. Information is distributed unevenly, so that each participant knows things that others do not and must decide what to share and what to withhold. Time pressure is introduced, not as an artificial constraint but as a reflection of the reality that most organizational negotiations occur under deadlines that do not permit unlimited exploration. And the simulation requires that the participants actually reach an agreement, which forces them to move past analysis and into the practical work of building alignment.

The simulation design should be drawn from the program's actual dynamics whenever possible. A simulation built around the program's real governance challenges, with roles that correspond to the actual stakeholder groups and interests that reflect the actual sources of friction, produces learning that is immediately transferable. The fictional overlay should be thin enough that participants recognize the dynamics but thick enough that they can experiment with approaches they might not attempt in a real conversation with a real stakeholder.

The debriefing of a simulation is where its value is realized. The facilitator should guide the discussion through a specific sequence. First, how were interests surfaced? Did the participants distinguish between positions and interests, or did the negotiation remain at the positional level? Second, how did framing shape the outcome? Were there moments where a different frame would have changed the dynamic? Third, what sequencing choices were made? Who was engaged first, and how did that sequence affect the conversations that followed? Fourth, where did the negotiation break down, and what would have prevented or recovered from the breakdown? This debriefing connects the simulation experience to the book's frameworks, reinforcing the concepts through reflection on lived experience rather than through abstract instruction.

Coaching as Sustained Development

Workshops and simulations build foundational competence. Coaching sustains and deepens that competence through ongoing, individualized support that is responsive to the specific challenges each leader encounters.

Pre-conversation coaching is the most immediately valuable form. Before a critical stakeholder meeting, a coaching conversation helps the change lead prepare by reviewing the Interest Map, testing the planned approach through scenario analysis, identifying the most likely points of resistance, and rehearsing specific language for difficult moments. The coaching session does not replace the leader's judgment. It sharpens it by providing a structured space for thinking through the conversation before it happens, which is a luxury that the pace of organizational life rarely affords without deliberate scheduling.

Post-conversation coaching extracts learning that might otherwise be lost. After a significant negotiation, a debriefing conversation reviews what happened, what the other party was responding to, where the approach worked, and where a different approach would have produced a better outcome. The debrief should be conducted with curiosity rather than evaluation. Its purpose is to build the leader's capacity for self-observation, the habit of noticing patterns in their own negotiation behavior that was described in Chapter 12. Over time, this habit becomes internalized, and the leader begins to debrief their own conversations without external support.

Mentoring relationships that pair experienced negotiators with emerging change leaders provide a different kind of development. Where coaching focuses on specific conversations and immediate skill application, mentoring addresses longer-term growth: how to read organizational dynamics, how to build relationships that support sustained negotiation over months and years, how to manage the emotional demands of work that involves constant engagement with other people's fears and concerns. The best mentoring relationships develop naturally from the workshop and coaching process, when a senior practitioner recognizes potential in a less experienced colleague and offers to share what they have learned through their own practice.

Tools as Cognitive Aids, Not Additional Process

The frameworks described throughout this book, Interest Maps, BATNA worksheets, stakeholder ecosystem maps, sequencing planners, framing templates, and the process design checklist from Chapter 13, are most valuable when they are treated as preparation aids rather than as documentation requirements. The distinction matters enormously for adoption. A tool that is perceived as an additional reporting obligation, another form to fill out and submit, will be resented and completed with minimal effort. A tool that is perceived as a genuine aid to preparation, something that makes a difficult conversation easier to navigate, will be used voluntarily and improved through practice.

The principle governing the integration of tools into organizational routines is that they should reduce the cognitive burden of applying negotiation thinking rather than adding to it. An Interest Map template that can be completed in fifteen minutes before a meeting, that prompts the leader to think through the key interests and their confidence levels, and that fits on a single page, is far more likely to be used than a comprehensive stakeholder analysis framework that requires hours of research and produces a document suitable for a governance archive. The tools should be lightweight, portable, and directly connected to the action they support. They should feel like checklists that a pilot reviews before a flight: not bureaucratic overhead but professional discipline that improves performance.

Embedding these tools into the organization's standard change management toolkit ensures their availability beyond any single program. When Interest Maps and sequencing planners are included in the organization's change methodology alongside the more familiar project plans and risk registers, they become part of the expected preparation for any significant initiative. Over time, their use normalizes. New change leaders encounter them as standard practice rather than as specialized techniques, and the negotiation capability that this book describes becomes a feature of how the organization operates rather than a quality that depends on the influence of a particular individual or the memory of a particular program.

The Negotiation Cycle: An End-to-End Model

The concepts and practices developed across the preceding chapters can be integrated into a single practical cycle that a change leader can follow through any phase of a transformation. The cycle is not a rigid sequence. It is a repeating loop, entered at whatever point corresponds to the current situation, that continues for as long as the transformation requires ongoing alignment.

The cycle begins with assessing the landscape. This means understanding how resistance operates in the specific organizational context (Chapter 2), mapping the stakeholder ecosystem with attention to informal power, coalition dynamics, and the cultural filters that shape how messages are received (Chapter 3), and identifying the early indicators of misalignment that suggest where alignment is weakening before the weakness becomes visible.

From the landscape assessment, the leader moves to mapping interests and alternatives. This involves applying the interests-versus-positions framework to each key stakeholder relationship (Chapter 4), building Interest Maps that capture confirmed, probable, and speculative interests (Chapter 5), and analyzing the BATNA, ZOPA, and leverage dynamics that define what is possible in each negotiation (Chapter 6).

With the mapping complete, the leader designs the engagement approach. This includes choosing the framing and influence strategy that is most likely to create the conditions for constructive engagement (Chapter 7), understanding the behavioral biases that may shape stakeholder responses and designing approaches that work with those biases rather than against them (Chapter 8), recognizing game-theoretic dynamics that may be producing coordination failures or equilibrium traps and designing structural interventions where appropriate (Chapter 9), and planning the sequencing and coalition-building strategy for multi-party negotiations (Chapter 10).

The leader then executes the engagement with adaptive style, drawing on the ability to shift between empathy, assertiveness, and analytical rigor depending on what each conversation requires (Chapter 12), and managing the crises that may arise when alignment is tested by unexpected pressure or failure (Chapter 11).

Throughout the process, the leader works to embed the outcomes in organizational processes, ensuring that the agreements reached and the alignment achieved are supported by incentive structures, governance mechanisms, and feedback loops that sustain them beyond the conversations that produced them (Chapter 13).

Finally, the leader learns from outcomes. Every negotiation, every stakeholder interaction, every crisis and recovery generates information about how the landscape has changed, which assumptions proved accurate, which interests shifted, and where the mapping needs to be updated. This learning feeds back into the landscape assessment, and the cycle begins again.

The cycle repeats because transformation is continuous. The landscape assessed in the first month of an initiative will be different in the sixth month, different again in the twelfth, and different still in the second year. Interests evolve. Coalitions reform. New pressures emerge. The cycle provides a discipline for staying current with these changes and for ensuring that the negotiation approach remains calibrated to the reality it is addressing rather than to the assumptions of an earlier phase.

Several patterns are worth watching for across cycles. Recurring resistance in the same area despite multiple interventions suggests that the structural conditions producing the resistance have not been addressed and that a process-level intervention may be needed. A widening gap between stated agreement and observable behavior indicates that the alignment is symbolic rather than genuine, and that the interest-mapping work needs to go deeper. Increasing stakeholder fatigue or declining engagement in governance forums signals that the negotiation demands on the organization may be exceeding its capacity to absorb them, and that the leader should simplify the engagement model rather than intensify it. A shift in which stakeholders are raising concerns, particularly when previously quiet groups become vocal, often indicates that the transformation has entered a new phase that activates different interests, and that the stakeholder map needs a thorough reassessment.

Closing Reflection

Negotiation is not a technique reserved for difficult moments or for specialized practitioners. It is a continuous leadership practice that sits at the center of how organizations move through change. Every transformation depends on alignment, and alignment is not a state to be achieved once and maintained passively. It is a condition that must be earned and re-earned through ongoing engagement with the interests, concerns, and aspirations of the people whose participation makes the work possible.

The tools and frameworks presented in these chapters are means to that end. Interest Maps, BATNA analysis, framing strategies, sequencing plans, and process design checklists are all instruments for understanding and engaging with the human dynamics that determine whether a transformation succeeds. But the instruments are only as effective as the disposition of the person using them. The leader who approaches stakeholder engagement with genuine curiosity about what others need, with honesty about what can and cannot be offered, and with the patience to let alignment develop at a pace that produces commitment rather than compliance, will find that the tools amplify a quality already present. The leader who applies the tools mechanically, without the underlying respect for the people on the other side of the conversation, will find that the techniques produce diminishing returns as stakeholders learn to recognize process without substance.

This is why the Preface described the work as "the quieter work of negotiation." It is quieter because it operates without public visibility, in conversations that unfold away from formal agendas and official records. It is quieter because it requires listening more than speaking, understanding more than persuading, and patience more than speed. And it is quieter because its success is measured not in dramatic breakthroughs but in the steady accumulation of trust, alignment, and shared commitment that allows an organization to move through uncertainty with confidence.

The capability to do this work can be taught, practiced, and sustained. It can be built into how organizations prepare for change, how they govern their programs, and how they develop their leaders. It is not the exclusive province of the naturally gifted negotiator. It is available to anyone willing to invest the attention that other people's concerns deserve and to develop the discipline that complex alignment requires. The organizations that build this capability will not merely manage their transformations more effectively. They will become, in a fundamental sense, more capable of operating as organizations, because the skills that sustain alignment through change are the same skills that sustain collaboration, trust, and shared purpose in every dimension of institutional life.

EPILOGUE

The ideas in this book did not begin as ideas. They began as situations. A meeting that should have produced agreement but did not. A stakeholder whose support was assumed and whose withdrawal was not anticipated. A program that had every structural advantage and still lost momentum, slowly, in the spaces between formal governance and actual commitment. Each of these experiences left something behind, not a lesson in the tidy sense, but a question that stayed open long enough to become useful.

Over time, those questions organized themselves into something that resembled a discipline. I began to notice that the conversations which changed the trajectory of a program shared certain qualities. They were patient. They treated the other person's concerns as legitimate even when those concerns were inconvenient. They moved past what was being said to engage with what was being protected or feared. And they were conducted by people who understood that the agreement they were building would need to survive contact with reality, which meant it had to be constructed from materials stronger than optimism or authority.

I also noticed that the programs which sustained their momentum over months and years were not the ones with the best strategies. They were the ones where the leaders closest to the work understood how to read the signals beneath the surface, how to detect when alignment was weakening before it fractured, and how to rebuild it without waiting for permission or crisis. These leaders were not always the most senior people in the room. They were the ones who paid the closest attention to the people around them and who treated that attention as a professional obligation rather than a personal preference.

This book has attempted to give structure to what those leaders do instinctively. The frameworks, the tables, the diagnostic tools, the worked examples are all efforts to make a set of practices visible and teachable that are often invisible precisely because they work. When a difficult negotiation is handled well, the result looks effortless. The conflict that did not escalate, the coalition that held, the stakeholder who shifted from skepticism to engagement, these outcomes leave no trace in the project record. They are experienced only by the people who were in the room, and often they are noticed only in retrospect, when someone realizes that a crisis was averted by a conversation they barely registered at the time.

I am under no illusion that a book can substitute for the experience of doing this work. The capacity to sit with someone's fear without rushing to resolve it, to hold a boundary without damaging a relationship, to recognize in the middle of a conversation that your approach is not working and to adjust without losing your footing, these are capacities that develop through practice and through the kind of reflection that only comes after you have gotten something wrong and taken the time to understand why. What a book can do is shorten the distance between early experience and useful insight, and provide a vocabulary for conversations that are otherwise difficult to discuss because they happen in the spaces that organizational language does not reach.

If this book has been useful to you, the evidence will not appear in how you think about transformation. It will appear in how you prepare for a conversation that matters. In the questions you ask before speaking. In the patience you bring to a stakeholder whose resistance you once would have dismissed. In your willingness to update your understanding of what someone needs, even when that understanding was hard-won and comfortable. The work of negotiation in transformation is never finished because the conditions it responds to are always changing. What can be finished, or at least begun, is the commitment to approach that work with the seriousness and the care it deserves.

I have been fortunate to do this work for many years, in environments that challenged and educated me in equal measure. The people I worked alongside, many of whom will not recognize themselves in these pages but whose influence is present throughout, taught me that the most consequential work in any organization is often the least visible. It happens in the conversation after the meeting. In the question that nobody else thought to ask. In the quiet decision to take someone's concerns seriously when it would have been easier not to. It is, as the preface of this book described it, the quieter work of negotiation. I hope these pages have helped you see that work more clearly and approach it with greater confidence.

Adolfo M. Carreno

APPENDICES

From Concept to Application

The preceding chapters have positioned strategic negotiation as an embedded capability within organizational transformation, shaping decisions, aligning stakeholders, and sustaining coherence under real operating conditions.

Understanding alone is insufficient. Execution introduces constraint, competing priorities, limited attention, and distributed decision authority. Within this environment, negotiation must operate as a disciplined practice, not as an abstract concept.

The appendices that follow are designed to support that transition.

They present a set of templates, tools, and playbooks intended to reduce ambiguity at critical decision points, reinforce consistency across stakeholders, and preserve coherence over time. They are not prescriptive instruments. Their value lies in how they are adapted and integrated into the specific context of the transformation effort.

In practice, these materials serve three functions: making assumptions and trade-offs explicit, structuring decision-making under pressure, and maintaining continuity across teams and phases of execution.

Editable versions of all materials are available, free of charge and exclusively for readers of this book, through the QR code below, and at **https://adolfocarreno.com/strategic-negotiation-toolbox/**

Appendix A
Tools and Templates

This appendix contains templates for the seven core frameworks developed in the book. Each template includes a brief instruction set and a reference to the chapter where the framework is introduced and explained in full. The templates are designed to be used as preparation aids before stakeholder conversations, not as reporting documents.

Tool 1: Interest Mapping Canvas

Reference: Chapters 4 and 5 - Interests vs. Positions; Mapping Interests

226

Instructions

Begin by recording the stakeholder's stated position at the center of the canvas. This is the explicit demand, request, or objection they have expressed. Then identify the interests that may explain the position, organized into four categories: functional, political, personal, and identity-based. For each interest, assign a confidence level: confirmed (stated directly or demonstrated consistently), probable (inferred from context or behavior), or speculative (a hypothesis requiring testing). Use the connections column to note relationships between interests. Update the canvas after each significant interaction.

Stakeholder: ____

Date: _______________ **Prepared by:** _______________________________

Stated Position:

Interest Category	Identified Interest	Confidence	Evidence / Source	Connections
Functional				
Functional				
Political				
Political				
Personal				
Personal				
Identity-Based				
Identity-Based				

Probing Questions for Next Conversation:

1.

2.

3.

Tool 2: BATNA Worksheet

Reference: Chapter 6 - Leverage, BATNA, and ZOPA Inside the Organization

Instructions

For each key stakeholder in the negotiation, identify their stated position, then assess what they would most likely do if no agreement is reached. This is their BATNA. Assess your own BATNA with the same rigor. Then estimate each party's tolerance range: the spectrum of outcomes they could accept. The gap between BATNAs defines the negotiation pressure. The overlap between tolerance ranges defines the ZOPA. Use this worksheet before any negotiation where the outcome is uncertain.

Your BATNA Assessment

What is your best alternative if this negotiation fails?
What are the costs and risks of exercising that alternative?
What is the minimum outcome you can accept before the alternative becomes preferable?

Stakeholder BATNA Analysis

Stakeholder	Stated Position	Likely BATNA	Estimated Tolerance Range	Implications for Strategy

Key observations:

Tool 3: ZOPA Analysis Chart

Reference: Chapter 6 - Leverage, BATNA, and ZOPA Inside the Organization

Instructions

The ZOPA Analysis Chart makes the zone of possible agreement visible. List the key interests at stake in the rows. List the options under consideration in the columns. For each cell, indicate whether the option fully satisfies ($\checkmark$), partially satisfies ($\sim$), or fails to address (X) the interest. The option that addresses the most interests with the fewest failures defines the center of the ZOPA. If no option adequately addresses all interests, the chart reveals where creative expansion is needed.

Negotiation Context

Issue: ____

Parties: ____

Trade-Off Matrix

Use √ = fully satisfies, ~ = partially satisfies, X = fails to address

Key Interest	Option A:	Option B:	Option C:	Option D:

ZOPA assessment: Where does the overlap exist? What creative options might expand it?

Tool 4: Stakeholder Ecosystem Map

Reference: Chapter 3 - Stakeholder Ecosystems: Power, Coalitions, and Shifting Ground

Instructions

Map each key stakeholder by category (supporter, skeptic, undecided), type of support or skepticism, and the informal networks through which their influence travels. Update this map regularly: before major governance meetings, after significant program events, and whenever informal signals suggest a shift in sentiment. Note hidden influencers who may not appear in formal stakeholder lists but whose opinions shape how others respond.

Program / Initiative: ____ **Date:** _________________

Stakeholder	Category	Type / Conditions	Key Interests	Influence Network	Trend

Category: Supporter (strong / conditional / symbolic) | Skeptic (practical / structural / experiential) | Undecided

Trend: Strengthening | Stable | Weakening | Unknown

Hidden influencers not listed above:

Coalition patterns observed:

Tool 5: Sequencing Planner

Reference: Chapter 10 - Sequencing, Coalitions, and Multi-Party Negotiation

Instructions

Use this planner to prepare for any multi-party negotiation or governance decision that requires pre-alignment. List stakeholders in the order you plan to engage them. For each, note their likely key interests, the specific goal of the conversation, what depends on prior conversations being completed first, and the risks or constraints you should be aware of. Complete this planner before the bilateral conversations begin, and update it after each conversation as the landscape shifts.

Decision / Meeting: _________________________________ **Date:** _______________

Order	Stakeholder	Key Interests	Goal of Conversation	Dependencies	Risks
1st					
2nd					
3rd					
4th					
5th					
Group					

Commitments tracker: Record every commitment made during bilateral conversations, however informal.

Made To	Commitment	Constrains Options For

Tool 6: Framing Template

Reference: Chapter 7 - Framing, Influence, and the Narratives That Move People

Instructions

Use this template to prepare the framing for any significant communication about the transformation. Begin by identifying the audience and their primary concerns. Draft the default frame (how the change would most naturally be described) and assess its likely reception. Then construct an alternative frame that addresses the same reality but is oriented toward what can be gained or protected rather than what will be lost. Test the frame against identity concerns: does it allow the audience to carry their professional identity forward, or does it require them to leave it behind?

Initiative / Change: ____

Audience: ____

Audience's primary concerns and interests

Default Frame	Alternative Frame
Why it may fail (what it activates)	Why it works (what it activates)

Identity check: Does the alternative frame allow the audience to carry their professional identity and expertise forward into the new environment?
Honesty check: Is the alternative frame accurate? Does it omit material facts? Are the promises keepable?

Chosen messenger and rationale:

Tool 7: Process Design Checklist

Reference: Chapter 13 - Designing Negotiation-Driven Processes

238

Instructions

Use this checklist when designing or reviewing governance processes for a transformation program. For each governance forum, assess whether negotiation elements have been embedded, whether the right information is being gathered beforehand, and whether the forum's outputs support sustained alignment. The checklist can also be used retrospectively to diagnose why a governance forum is producing adversarial dynamics rather than collaborative outcomes.

Program: ____ **Date:** ___________________

Governance Forum	Negotiation Elements Embedded	Information Gathered Beforehand	Outputs Produced
Steering Committee			
Program Review			
Working Group			
Escalation Forum			
Other:			

Structural Assessment

Question	Yes	No	Action Needed
Do incentive structures reward collaborative behavior?			
Are shared metrics in place for jointly accountable outcomes?			
Do governance forums allocate time for interest exploration before decisions?			
Are escalation paths pre-agreed with clear triggers?			
Do escalation processes require interest mapping alongside factual summaries?			
Are feedback channels credible (i.e., acted upon visibly)?			
Is there a structured process for raising and resolving concerns?			
Does recognition value collective contribution alongside individual performance?			

Priority adjustments identified:

Appendix B
Diagnostic Checklists

This appendix contains four diagnostic checklists designed for use during active transformation programs. Each checklist maps to a specific chapter and is structured for rapid assessment: scan the indicators, check those that are present, note the implications, and identify the response. These are field instruments, not comprehensive analyses. They are most useful when consulted regularly and when the patterns they reveal are acted upon promptly.

Checklist 1: Resistance Pattern Checklist

Reference: Chapter 2, The Anatomy of Resistance

242

Use this checklist to assess whether resistance patterns are forming within a stakeholder group, a function, or across the program. Review at regular intervals and after any significant program event. Patterns that cluster together indicate systemic resistance that requires structural engagement, not communication.

Program / Team assessed: _________________________________ **Date:** ____________

Quiet Refusal Indicators

✓	Indicator	What It Suggests	Notes / Evidence
☐	Tasks completed in the narrowest possible sense; rework frequently required.	Participation is formal but engagement is withheld. The team is complying without committing.	
☐	Follow-up actions from meetings are acknowledged but not prioritized or completed.	Stated agreement is not translating into behavioral change. Concerns may be unresolved.	
☐	Meetings end with apparent agreement but produce little practical movement afterward.	Surface consensus is masking underlying hesitation. Bilateral follow-up is needed.	
☐	Offers of additional support are met with polite but vague responses.	The team may be managing the program's attention rather than engaging with it.	

Symbolic Agreement Indicators

✓	Indicator	What It Suggests	Notes / Evidence
☐	Stakeholders endorse the strategy but resist specific implications for their own area.	Support is at the level of principle, not commitment. The position has not been tested by concrete demands.	
☐	Parallel processes or legacy practices continue alongside the new model.	The formal sign-off was treated as the end of obligation rather than the beginning of adoption.	
☐	Verbal alignment in governance forums contrasts with informal skepticism reported through other channels.	Public and private positions diverge. The governance forum may not be a safe space for honest engagement.	

Passive Drift Indicators

✓	Indicator	What It Suggests	Notes / Evidence
☐	Early enthusiasm has dissolved into routine execution; tasks are completed without connection to purpose.	Momentum has weakened without a triggering event. Competing priorities or unclear incentives may be displacing the transformation.	
☐	Goals have become abstract; teams describe their work in operational terms rather than transformation terms.	The narrative connecting daily work to the larger change has faded. Re-engagement at the purpose level is needed.	
☐	Progress metrics remain acceptable but qualitative engagement has declined.	Compliance is maintained but discretionary effort has withdrawn. The transformation is surviving rather than advancing.	

Early Misalignment Indicators

✓	Indicator	What It Suggests	Notes / Evidence
☐	Different teams describe the same directive in meaningfully different terms.	Shared understanding has not been established. Concerns are filtering interpretation.	
☐	Decision-making has slowed; justifications for delay are vague or circular.	Hesitations are forming beneath the surface. Hidden concerns require exploration.	
☐	Stakeholders increasingly reference policy, precedent, or procedure rather than engaging with new expectations.	Anchoring to the familiar as a response to uncertainty. Conversations need to shift toward intent and rationale.	
☐	Inconsistent narratives about the program's purpose or urgency across functions or regions.	Fragmentation is increasing. Unified engagement and targeted clarification are needed before divergence widens.	

Overall assessment and priority actions:

Checklist 2: Stakeholder Sentiment Indicators

Reference: Chapter 3, Stakeholder Ecosystems: Power, Coalitions, and Shifting Ground

Use this checklist to assess whether stakeholder sentiment is shifting. Review before major governance meetings and after significant program events. Focus particularly on movement among the undecided, on changes in coalition composition, and on any divergence between formal positions and informal signals.

Program: ____ **Date:** _______________

Review period since: _________________

Support Quality Indicators

✓	Signal	Possible Meaning	Affected Stakeholder(s)	Recommended Response
☐	A previously strong supporter has become less vocal or less engaged in governance forums.	Support may be weakening; new concerns may have emerged or competing pressures are diverting attention.		Schedule a bilateral conversation to understand what has changed.
☐	Conditional supporters are testing whether their conditions are being met.	The conditions attached to support are becoming active. Failure to honor them risks withdrawal.		Review commitments made; confirm progress visibly.
☐	Support from one stakeholder is increasingly symbolic: public endorsement without substantive engagement.	The gap between stated and actual commitment is widening. The support may not survive a concrete test.		Engage directly on what specific participation looks like; surface any hidden concerns.

Skepticism and Opposition Indicators

✓	Signal	Possible Meaning	Affected Stakeholder(s)	Recommended Response
☐	A previously neutral stakeholder has begun raising concerns or asking sharper questions.	New information, informal conversations, or pressure from their own team may be shifting their stance.		Explore the source of the shift; address specific concerns before the position hardens.
☐	Skeptics are using increasingly similar language across different conversations.	Informal communication has produced a shared narrative. A coalition may be forming or consolidating.		Identify the most reasonable skeptic and engage first; address the shared concern directly.
☐	A stakeholder is requesting bilateral conversations rather than engaging through governance forums.	Concerns have become specific enough to require private discussion. This may be a positive signal if engaged well.		Accept the request promptly; treat it as an opportunity for interest exploration.

Undecided and Coalition Indicators

✓	Signal	Possible Meaning	Affected Stakeholder(s)	Recommended Response
☐	Undecided stakeholders are observing early results closely but have not yet committed.	Their decision depends on the evidence produced by early phases. They represent the next wave of alignment or resistance.		Ensure early results are visible and well-communicated; provide direct access to early adopters.
☐	Informal networks are carrying a narrative that differs from official program messaging.	The informal narrative is likely more influential than the official one. Ignoring it will not make it disappear.		Engage with the informal narrative directly through trusted intermediaries and informal channels.
☐	Coalition boundaries are shifting: previously separate groups are coordinating or previously aligned groups are fragmenting.	The stakeholder landscape is restructuring. The ecosystem map needs immediate revision.		Update the stakeholder ecosystem map; reassess sequencing and engagement priorities.
☐	A hidden influencer's position has shifted, with ripple effects across their network.	Informal influence is reshaping the landscape. Formal governance may not reflect the change.		Engage the influencer directly and understand their new position; assess network implications.

Summary: Key shifts since last review and priority engagements:

Checklist 3: Behavioral Bias Recognition Guide

Reference: Chapter 8, Behavioral Bias in Change: Why Rational Plans Meet Irrational Resistance

Use this guide when stakeholder behavior seems disproportionate to the operational circumstances, or when well-supported proposals meet resistance that cannot be explained by the stated objections. Check each bias that may be active, note the specific evidence, and identify the corresponding response. Multiple biases typically operate simultaneously, and the combination produces a qualitatively different kind of resistance than any single bias alone.

Situation assessed: _________________________________ **Date:** ___________

✓	Bias	Behavioral Signals Present	Evidence in This Situation	Practical Response
☐	Status Quo Bias	Preference for existing processes despite demonstrated alternatives; continued use of workarounds after new processes are available; reluctance to abandon familiar tools.		Make the first step small and reversible. Preserve familiar elements during early phases. Allow coexistence temporarily.
☐	Loss Aversion	Disproportionate focus on what will be lost; stronger emotional response to potential losses than equivalent gains; reluctance to commit despite favorable analysis.		Frame in terms of what is gained or protected. Ensure early experiences deliver visible, tangible benefits before demanding full commitment.
☐	Identity Threat	Defensive objections persisting after operational concerns are addressed; resistance concentrated among the most skilled practitioners of the current approach; arguments that the change is unnecessary rather than unworkable.		Position existing expertise as essential to the transition. Create roles that carry forward current knowledge. Acknowledge contributions before describing what comes next.

☐	Loss of Control	Resistance from intellectually supportive individuals; focus on process objections; demands for more information, review, or time before committing.	Involve affected individuals in shaping implementation before announcing decisions. Provide genuine input opportunities within defined parameters.
☐	Confirmation Bias	Selective attention to negative signals; dismissal of positive evidence; progressive hardening of skepticism without new justifying events.	Invest in early positive experiences. Introduce disconfirming evidence through trusted peers and direct experience rather than argument.
☐	Emotional Reactivity	Anxiety, frustration, or withdrawal disproportionate to the operational implications; difficulty engaging with analytical content during transformation discussions.	Begin with acknowledgment and validation. Address the emotional reality before attempting to reframe. Earn the right to offer a different perspective.

Interaction Pattern

When multiple biases are checked above, note how they may be reinforcing each other. For example, status quo bias combined with confirmation bias produces a self-reinforcing loop where familiarity is preferred and evidence supporting the new approach is discounted. Identity threat combined with loss of control produces defensive behavior that is both emotionally intense and procedurally obstructive.

Observed interaction pattern:

Adjusted response strategy:

Checklist 4: Crisis Alignment Checklist

Reference: Chapter 11, Crisis Negotiation: Maintaining Alignment Under Pressure

Use this checklist in the immediate aftermath of a significant disruption: a system failure, a missed milestone, an unexpected stakeholder withdrawal, or any event that shakes confidence in the program. The checklist guides the two parallel tracks of crisis response: addressing the operational issue and rebuilding the stakeholder alignment that the crisis has damaged. Complete within 48 to 72 hours of the triggering event.

Crisis event: ____ **Date:** ________________

Immediate Assessment (First 24 Hours)

✓	Action	Purpose	Status / Notes
☐	Establish the facts: what happened, what is the operational impact, and what is the current status of containment or resolution.	A clear factual account prevents speculation from filling the vacuum. The leader must know the facts before communicating.	
☐	Identify which stakeholders have been directly affected and which are likely to learn about the crisis through informal channels.	Stakeholders who hear about the crisis from sources other than the program team will form interpretations outside the program's influence.	
☐	Assess which stakeholders' support was conditional and whether the crisis has activated the conditions for withdrawal.	Conditional support is most vulnerable during crises. Identifying at-risk relationships early allows for targeted intervention.	
☐	Determine whether any stakeholder's informal influence has shifted as a result of the crisis (gained or lost credibility).	Crises redistribute influence. Someone who acted decisively gains standing; someone who is perceived as responsible loses it.	

Stakeholder Re-engagement (24 to 72 Hours)

✓	Action	Purpose	Status / Notes
☐	Communicate directly with the executive sponsor: provide a clear factual account, acknowledge the impact honestly, and outline next steps.	The sponsor needs a narrative they can use with their own leadership. Honesty and specificity build credibility; minimization erodes it.	
☐	Re-assess each key stakeholder's BATNA: what is their most likely alternative to continued participation now that the crisis has occurred?	BATNAs shift during crises. Passive non-compliance, escalation, and withdrawal all become more attractive when confidence is shaken.	
☐	Initiate bilateral conversations with the most at-risk stakeholders, beginning with those whose withdrawal would have the greatest impact.	Waiting for stakeholders to raise their concerns in a governance forum makes recovery harder. Early private engagement preserves flexibility.	
☐	Ask each stakeholder: "What do you need right now?" rather than "How do we get back on track?"	The first question accepts that the landscape has changed. The second assumes the pre-crisis plan is still the correct destination.	
☐	Acknowledge any individual or team whose actions during the crisis were correct (e.g., reverting to a stable system), regardless of whether those actions were authorized.	Failing to acknowledge good judgment during a crisis alienates people who have gained informal credibility through their response.	

Rebuilding Alignment (First Two Weeks)

✓	Action	Purpose	Status / Notes
☐	Propose a new short-term agreement that is modest enough to be credible given the current level of stakeholder trust.	Ambitious commitments made in the aftermath of a crisis will not be believed. Modest, keepable commitments begin rebuilding credibility.	
☐	Deliver on every commitment made during the crisis response, including small ones, visibly and on time.	Every kept promise accumulates credibility. Every missed promise, however minor, confirms the narrative of unreliability.	
☐	Update the stakeholder ecosystem map and Interest Maps to reflect the post-crisis landscape.	The pre-crisis maps are no longer accurate. Interests have shifted, power has redistributed, and coalition dynamics have changed.	
☐	Conduct a post-crisis review focused on what the crisis revealed about the quality of pre-crisis alignment.	Crises reveal which agreements were fragile, which support was conditional, and where the mapping was incomplete. This is actionable intelligence.	
☐	Resist the temptation to restore the status quo ante. Use post-crisis clarity to build something stronger than what existed before.	Agreements built on tested understanding are more durable than agreements built on untested assumptions.	

Post-crisis lessons and adjustments to the negotiation approach:

Appendix C
Scenario Playbooks

The following three scenarios illustrate the negotiation cycle described in Chapter 14, applied end-to-end to situations that recur across transformation programs. Each playbook walks through the full sequence: assessing the landscape, mapping interests and alternatives, designing the engagement approach, executing with adaptive style, embedding outcomes in process, and learning from results. The scenarios are composites drawn from common transformation patterns. They are intended as worked references, not prescriptive templates.

Scenario 1: Standardization Friction

Cross-functional conflict during process standardization

A global consumer goods company undertook a standardization of its demand planning process across four regional business units. The corporate supply chain team designed a unified planning model that would replace four regional approaches with a single framework, supported by a shared technology platform. The business case was strong: reduced forecast error, lower inventory carrying costs, and improved visibility across the network. The executive committee approved the initiative with the expectation that all regions would adopt the standard model within eighteen months.

Assess. Within the first two months, two of the four regional heads expressed concerns. The European head questioned whether the global model could accommodate the regulatory complexity of planning across multiple EU markets. The Latin American head argued that his region's demand volatility required a level of local judgment that the standardized model would constrain. The Asian and North American heads were cautiously supportive but noncommittal. A review of the stakeholder landscape revealed that the European and Latin American heads were not coordinating their positions but had arrived at similar concerns independently, a pattern consistent with parallel rather than coalition-based resistance. The program team also identified two hidden influencers: a senior demand planner in Europe whose technical opinion was widely respected, and a supply chain director in Latin America who had lived through a failed standardization attempt three years earlier and whose skepticism carried significant weight among his peers.

Map. Interest mapping revealed that the European head's stated position, requesting a regional exception, was driven by a combination of functional interests (genuine regulatory complexity that the standard model had not fully addressed) and identity-based interests (the European planning team had built a methodology they considered superior to the global average, and the standardization felt like a demotion of their expertise). The Latin American head's position was rooted in experiential skepticism from the prior failure, compounded by a personal interest in protecting his team from another costly transition that might be reversed. BATNA analysis showed that both regional heads' most likely alternative to agreement was passive non-compliance: adopting the system formally while continuing to run local processes in parallel. The program team's BATNA was a phased rollout starting with the two supportive regions, using their results to build the case for broader adoption.

Design. The engagement approach combined framing and sequencing. The program team reframed the initiative from "replacing regional processes with a global standard" to "building a common foundation that incorporates the strongest elements from each region's methodology." This frame protected the identity of the European team by positioning their expertise as a contribution rather than a casualty. The sequencing plan engaged the North American head first, secured her commitment, then engaged the Asian head with evidence of North American support, and approached the two skeptical regions with a coalition already in place. The European demand planner was engaged as a technical advisor to the design team, which converted a hidden influencer from potential skeptic to active participant.

Execute. Bilateral conversations with the European head explored the regulatory concern in detail and produced a specific set of accommodations within the standard model that addressed the legitimate complexity without creating a full exception. The conversation required a blend of empathy, to acknowledge the identity concern, and analysis, to work through the technical requirements. The Latin American conversation was harder. The experiential skepticism required patience and the explicit acknowledgment that the previous failure had been real and costly. The program director offered a structured review mechanism that gave the Latin American head a formal exit point if the implementation failed to meet defined performance thresholds within six months, which addressed the fear of being trapped in another failing initiative.

Embed. The governance structure was modified to include a regional advisory panel that reviewed the model's performance quarterly and recommended adjustments. This mechanism addressed the ongoing concern about local responsiveness and prevented the standardization from becoming a rigid imposition that would generate recurring friction. Shared metrics were introduced that measured forecast accuracy at both the global and regional level, so that regional teams were recognized for their contribution to the enterprise result rather than only measured against a standard they did not design.

Learn. The post-implementation review revealed that the most effective intervention was not any single conversation but the structural decision to involve regional expertise in the design process. The European demand planner's participation not only improved the model but signaled to the broader organization that standardization did not mean centralization of judgment. The Latin American review mechanism was never invoked, but its existence provided the psychological safety that enabled genuine adoption rather than performative compliance.

Scenario 2: Technology Adoption Resistance

Team-level resistance to a new operational platform

A mid-sized insurance company introduced a new claims processing platform to replace a legacy system that had been in use for twelve years. The platform offered significant improvements in processing speed, data quality, and reporting capability. The implementation team had successfully deployed the system in two regional offices. The third office, the largest and most experienced claims operation in the company, was where adoption stalled.

Assess. The team at the third office consisted of forty claims processors, many of whom had spent their entire careers on the legacy system. Their manager, a well-respected operations leader with eighteen years of tenure, had attended all preparatory briefings and expressed support for the initiative. Yet three months after go-live, fewer than half of her team's claims were being processed through the new platform. The remainder were still being handled through the legacy system, which had been left running in parallel for the transition period. Diagnostic indicators were present: tasks completed to minimum standards, questions not being raised in training sessions, and informal feedback suggesting that the team viewed the new system as slower and more cumbersome than the one it replaced.

Map. Interest mapping of the team manager revealed a confirmed functional interest in maintaining processing throughput during a period when the team was already under pressure from a seasonal claims surge. A probable identity-based interest was also evident: she had built her reputation on the team's processing efficiency, and the transition-period slowdown threatened that reputation. Among the senior processors, the dominant interest was personal: fear that the new system would expose the limits of their technical skills, since their expertise was deeply embedded in the legacy platform's specific workflows. BATNA analysis showed that the team's most likely alternative was indefinite parallel processing, which technically complied with the rollout but ensured the legacy system remained the de facto operational standard.

Design. The framing strategy positioned the team's legacy expertise as an asset rather than an obsolescence risk: "Your understanding of claims complexity is exactly what we need to configure the new platform for the cases that matter most. The system handles the routine work; your judgment handles the exceptions." This frame protected identity while creating a role for the team in shaping the new system's configuration. The engagement sequencing targeted three senior processors who were identified as informal opinion leaders within the team, engaging them in a configuration workshop before addressing the broader team.

Execute. The configuration workshop produced two results. First, it surfaced specific workflow gaps in the new platform that the implementation team had not anticipated, which the senior processors were able to identify because of their deep domain knowledge. Addressing these gaps improved the platform's functionality for the entire company, which was communicated as a direct contribution from the third office's expertise. Second, the workshop gave the three senior processors hands-on experience with the system in a low-pressure environment, which reduced their personal anxiety about capability and gave them a credible basis for encouraging their peers. The team manager was engaged separately with a temporary performance protection arrangement: her team's processing metrics during the transition would be assessed against an adjusted baseline that accounted for the learning curve, protecting her reputation during the period of highest vulnerability.

Embed. The parallel processing arrangement was given a defined sunset date, communicated transparently as a transition tool rather than a permanent option. A weekly feedback channel was established through which the team could report platform issues directly to the implementation team, with a commitment to visible response within forty-eight hours. This channel addressed the ongoing concern about being heard and ensured that the team's experience continued to influence the platform's development.

Learn. The key insight was that the stalled adoption was not a technology problem or a training problem. It was an interest problem: the team's core concerns, about capability exposure, reputational risk, and the loss of domain expertise as a source of professional value, were not addressed by the standard implementation approach, which focused on functionality and training. Once those interests were identified and engaged, the adoption timeline compressed significantly. The configuration workshop model was subsequently adopted as a standard element of the platform's rollout to remaining offices.

Scenario 3: Cross-Functional Priority Conflict

Multi-party negotiation over competing transformation workstreams

A financial services firm was running three transformation workstreams simultaneously: a customer experience redesign led by the commercial function, a core systems modernization led by technology, and an operational efficiency program led by operations. Each workstream had executive sponsorship, a dedicated budget, and an approved timeline. The conflict emerged when all three workstreams required the same pool of business analysts during the same quarter, and the available capacity was sufficient for approximately two of the three.

Assess. The landscape assessment revealed a classic coordination failure compounded by structural incentive misalignment. Each workstream lead was measured on their own program's milestones and had no incentive to yield capacity to a peer workstream. The governance structure included a portfolio steering committee, but its quarterly cadence was too slow to resolve a real-time resource conflict, and its decision rights over individual workstream staffing were ambiguous. The three leads had each escalated the issue to their respective sponsors, producing three competing executive requests to the COO, whose involvement risked politicizing what was fundamentally a coordination problem.

Map. Interest mapping revealed that the commercial lead's primary interest was time-to-market: the customer experience redesign had a competitive window that would close if delayed beyond the quarter. The technology lead's primary interest was architectural integrity: the systems modernization had reached a phase where deferring the analytical work would create technical debt that would cost significantly more to address later. The operations lead's primary interest was team credibility: her workstream had already been delayed once, and a second delay would undermine confidence in the program and, by extension, in her leadership. None of these interests was illegitimate. The ZOPA appeared narrow because the resource pool was fixed, but creative options existed if the problem could be reframed beyond a single quarter.

Design. The engagement approach involved reframing the problem from "who gets the analysts this quarter" to "how do we sequence the analytical work across the three programs to protect each program's most critical interests." The sequencing plan engaged the operations lead first, because her interest, credibility protection, was the most addressable without requiring resource concessions. A public commitment from the portfolio steering committee that her program's revised timeline reflected a deliberate sequencing decision rather than a failure of execution would address the reputational concern. The commercial and technology leads were then engaged jointly, with a proposal to split the analyst pool between them for the current quarter and to give the operations program priority access in the following quarter, creating a rotation that distributed the benefit across time rather than concentrating the cost on one party.

Execute. The bilateral conversation with the operations lead required empathy: she had been through one delay already and was understandably wary of being asked to absorb another. The program director acknowledged the cost directly and proposed the public steering committee statement as a concrete commitment. The joint conversation with the commercial and technology leads required analysis: both needed to see the sequencing logic clearly and to understand that the proposed split, while imperfect, protected each program's most critical interest better than any winner-take-all resolution. The technology lead initially pushed for full allocation, arguing that the technical debt risk justified priority. The program director held the line by referencing the commercial lead's time-to-market constraint and by showing, through a simple trade-off matrix, that partial allocation to both programs preserved more collective value than full allocation to either.

Embed. The resolution exposed a structural gap in the governance framework: the portfolio steering committee had no mechanism for resolving real-time resource conflicts across workstreams. A lightweight arbitration process was designed and adopted, with clear triggers for activation, defined decision criteria, and a commitment to resolution within five business days. Shared portfolio-level metrics were introduced alongside individual workstream metrics, so that each lead had visibility into and accountability for the overall portfolio's performance, not only their own program's milestones.

Learn. The most significant learning was that the conflict was predictable and preventable. The three workstreams had been planned independently, with no cross-portfolio resource analysis. The arbitration process addressed the symptom, but the deeper lesson was about portfolio design: when multiple programs share a constrained resource pool, the coordination mechanism must be designed into the governance structure from the outset, not improvised after the conflict has escalated. The experience was used to redesign the firm's portfolio planning process to include a resource interdependency assessment as a standard step.

These three scenarios illustrate the negotiation cycle at different organizational levels: cross-functional (standardization), team-level (technology adoption), and multi-party portfolio (priority conflict). In each case, the resolution depended not on a single intervention but on the integrated application of interest mapping, BATNA analysis, framing, sequencing, and process design. The scenarios are intentionally detailed enough to serve as preparation references for readers facing similar situations, and intentionally general enough to be adapted to the specific dynamics of their own organizations. For the underlying frameworks referenced in each scenario, consult the relevant chapters and the templates in Appendix A.

www.ingramcontent.com/pod-product-compliance
Lightning Source LLC
Chambersburg PA
CBHW041306120726
48005CB00014B/1882